Artful Teaching

INTEGRATING THE ARTS
FOR UNDERSTANDING
ACROSS THE CURRICULUM, K–8

Edited by
David M. Donahue
Jennifer Stuart

Foreword by
Cyrus E. Driver

Afterword by
Lois Hetland

Teachers College, Columbia University
New York and London

National Art Education
Association

Published simultaneously by Teachers College Press, 1234 Amsterdam Avenue, New York, NY 10027 and the National Art Education Association, 1916 Association Drive, Reston, VA 20191

Library of Congress Cataloging-in-Publication Data

Artful teaching : integrating the arts for understanding across the curriculum, K–8 / edited by David M. Donahue, Jennifer Stuart ; foreword by Cyrus E. Driver ; Afterword by Lois Hetland.
      p. cm.
   Includes bibliographical references and index.
   ISBN 978-0-8077-5080-3 (pbk. : alk. paper) — ISBN 978-0-8077-5081-0 (hardcover : alk. paper)   1. Art—Study and teaching—United States.   2. Art and society—United States.
I. Donahue, David M.   II. Stuart, Jennifer.
   LB159.5.U6I67 2010
   372.5—dc22

                                                                      2010008914

ISBN 978-0-8077-5080-3 (paperback)
ISBN 978-0-8077-5081-0 (hardcover)

Printed on acid-free paper
Manufactured in the United States of America

17   16   15   14   13   12   11   10   8   7   6   5   4   3   2   1

Contents

Foreword

THE FORD FOUNDATION launched Integrating the Arts and Education Reform (ArtsEd), an initiative designed to bring high-quality arts integration to scale across America's urban public schools, in 2003. ArtsEd sought to demonstrate the power of the arts to transform our cities' public schools by making student imagination, creativity, and voice central to learning.

At the time, the powerful standards and accountability movement was already narrowing public school curricula and instructional practices. Nowhere were the pernicious effects of these efforts, which continue to this day, more evident than in the public schools of big cities serving almost exclusively children of color from low-income families. The ArtsEd initiative was developed in response to this aggressive movement.

Foundation staff recognized that 21st-century American work and life demanded skills and attributes such as creativity, flexibility, and authentic respect for difference, which the arts are particularly powerful in cultivating. We viewed integration of the arts in our schools as a key element in students' future opportunity and success, while the predominant educational policies were taking our schools and students in exactly the opposite direction. ArtsEd was designed to push back against this policy landscape by demonstrating the educational benefits of integrating arts education at scale in cities, including Dallas; Cleveland; Baltimore; and Jackson, Miss., as well as in districts in California's San Francisco Bay Area, such as Oakland, Emery, and Berkeley.

Over the course of the initiative, we also came to understand more clearly how access to quality arts education in general, and to arts integration in particular, was not just a matter of access, but a central issue of equity in our public schools. Arts integration can help enrich learning, but more important, the practice can, as Richard Deasy, former director of the Arts Education Partnership, says, *democratize* classrooms—enabling each student's voice and perspective to be represented on equal terms through their artistic expressions.

As the foundation began to support projects across the country to bring arts integration to our city's public schools, we encountered numerous kindred spirits—educators, families, policymakers, business and civic leaders, and artists—who believed that the arts should be central to a quality public education. Many such like-minded visionaries are among this volume's authors. Several of the authors have actually been Ford grantees through their involvement in the two Bay Area projects we funded.

Yet the field of arts integration remains quite nascent in its development both theoretically and in practice. How arts integration contributes to student learning and development must be better understood and explained by its advocates. This volume takes steps to address these shortcomings in two ways.

First, the rich and lively chapters may be read as "stories" of how integrated arts education functions in classrooms when done well. The chapters provide case studies based on the experiences of arts integration educators in public school classrooms across the Bay Area. The chapters also explore intensive teacher education and principal training programs now under way in several higher-education institutions in the region. When read this way, the chapters should be of interest and value to anyone who is engaged in urban education reform at the school, district, or policy levels.

The second way that the chapters can be read is as "practitioner guides," to help teachers and principals better understand and carry out arts integration in their own classrooms and schools. The chapters offer concrete ideas and heuristics for educators who are looking to strengthen their own skills, experience, and ability to improve student opportunities for learning.

Educators are increasingly taking heart and taking hold of arts integration in the ways described in this wonderful volume. As families and city leaders begin to observe the transformative effects of arts-integrated schools, it is my hope that the arts gain further traction in our schools, and ultimately become a fundamental part of basic public education.

Cyrus E. Driver

Five Best Questions About Arts Integration

What to Ask Before You Start

David M. Donahue and Jennifer Stuart
(with Todd Elkin and Arzu Mistry)

TEACHERS, school leaders, and educational researchers love the phrase "best practices." A search of the ERIC (Education Resources Information Center) database in early 2008 yielded over 1,600 results describing "best practices" for everything from literacy instruction and school meal programs to boater safety education and disciplinary alternative schools. The term "best practices" has great currency because it implies action, efficiency, and something that will work everywhere at all times. The search for such practices has a long history in U.S. education (Tyack & Cuban, 1997).

As teachers interested in arts integration, we have our own "best practices." The authors in this volume, for example, share exemplary arts integration practices across the K–8 curriculum. But rather than present them as panaceas appropriate in all contexts with all students, they carefully describe how the arts provide an entry point for gaining insight into why and how students learn. They do not provide formulas or scripts to be implemented with fidelity to any program. In that sense, they are "teaching against the grain" (Cochran-Smith, 1991) of standardized schools and formulaic curriculum. They see value in knowing students as individuals and as a classroom community. They want to make schools more equitable places of learning for all students, including students in urban schools where scripted curricula in reading and math limit understanding; divorce content and teaching from local contexts and students' needs and strengths; and stifle teacher and student creativity, flexibility, and originality—conditions that, by contrast, the arts encourage (Eisner, 2002; Fowler, 1996; Hoffman Davis, 2008, Rabkin, 2004). Integrating the arts into the curriculum reminds us that "teaching is as much a personal performance, a moral endeavor, and a cultural script as it is a technical craft" (Gay & Kirkland, 2003, p. 182). Instead of one best system, the arts provide a "third space" (Stevenson & Deasy, 2005) for learning by students and teachers.

A third space is the place where meaning exists in art, not in the viewer alone or the piece of art itself, but somewhere in the relationship between the two where the viewer brings past knowledge, experiences, and imagination to make meaning from a work of art. Similarly, those making art enter a third space as they combine their knowledge, experiences, and imagination with the materials and methods of an art form to create pieces that hold meaning and invite viewers to create meaning. In this third space, students and teachers find what the director-general of UNESCO, Koïchiro Matsuura, called "the promise of unexpected dialogues" (Mbuyamba, 2006, p. 3).

In the spirit of these unexpected dialogues, we open this book with five "best questions" about arts integration to ask before, during, and after engaging in arts-integrated practice. We believe these questions have salience for educators in settings from kindergarten through middle school and beyond and pose them as reference points for your reflection while reading this book.

While the prescribed curriculum and standardized testing that dominate schools in the name of standards would seem to preclude the need for teachers to raise questions and reflect, what changes in such a climate is not the need to reflect, but the nature of the questions (Donahue, 2005). Such prescribed curriculum and standardized testing limit understanding by asking questions with only one "right" answer. Consequently the following questions in this chapter take on even greater importance. In providing our own preliminary responses to these questions, we make no presumption about best practices. Rather, we hope our thinking will invite you into unexpected dialogues in the third space. Toward that goal, we end the discussion of each question with further related questions. The authors of each chapter that follows have their own answers to these. They offer their thinking, not to prescribe answers, but to widen our perspective.

This is a "workbook," in the sense that the authors ask you, the reader, to engage in reflection and various thought exercises as you read. In some cases, they will ask you to reflect on your experiences making or looking at art or the assumptions behind your ideas of what qualifies as art. In other cases, they will ask you to think about your teaching and the opportunities that already exist for integrating the arts into your practice. Other authors ask you to think about the potential partners for arts integration and the resources in your community on which you can draw. While *Artful Teaching* is full of suggestions and ideas, it is full of questions as well. One of the benefits of arts integration is the way it encourages stretching and exploring in our thinking. We hope this book pushes you in the same direction as well.

WHY INTEGRATE THE ARTS?

Before coming up with a rationale for arts integration, ask yourself, "What do the arts mean in my life?" Considering some recent experiences might be helpful here. Think about the last play or concert you attended or a recent experience onstage or playing a musical instrument. Picture a painting or poster on your walls or the last time you worked on a mural or collage. Now write 10 words that describe what your own particular experience with art means to you. Or, better yet, sketch a symbol capturing that experience's meaning. At the same time, note how your understanding of the experience is shaped by the very act of representing it visually. Perhaps you're already experiencing new reasons for integrating the arts in your curriculum. Or perhaps you're realizing the thought and preparation required for meaningful arts integration. While you are realizing the scaffolding required for arts integration, you are probably also realizing how much you already know about symbols and how symbols and art are already a part of your life.

Ask at least four other people to do the same and share their symbols or lists with you. Talk to people who differ from you in age, race, culture, or educational level. You are not conducting a scientific survey, but you want to see the meaning of the arts for people from diverse backgrounds. If you are working with colleagues at school to integrate the arts, try this as a group exercise.

You probably found that the meaning of art for you and others varied. Similarly, arts advocates vary in their reasons for integrating the arts. In addition to being valuable in their own right (Hoffman Davis, 2008), the arts are seen as fostering improved learning in other subject areas (Fiske, 1999). They also further students' cognitive abilities (Efland, 2002; Gardner, 1993; Perkins, 1994), promote creative self-expression (Lowenfeld, 1947), transform consciousness and imagination (Eisner, 2002; Greene, 1995), and promote multicultural understanding and social justice (Bains & Mesa-Bains, 2002; Heck, 2001).

While the scientific evidence of transfer to learning in other subject areas is thin (Hetland & Winner, 2001) and the justification of the arts in the curriculum as an aid to learning something else is problematic because it can reduce art to a "handmaiden," any and all of the other reasons for integrating the arts have merit. At the same time, the arts are not able to accomplish any or all of these goals solely by virtue of their integration in the curriculum. In line with the maxim "Less is more" (Blythe, 1997), curricular goals for arts integration should be few and explicit. Looking at those lists of 10 words or reflecting on the symbols you and others drew, what are one or two key reasons why you want to integrate the arts?

In our own teaching of preservice teachers, we have used the "studio habits of mind" (Hetland, Winner, Veenema, & Sheridan, 2007) to provide a theoretical underpinning for integrating the arts because we believe they capture the kinds of thinking we value but see underutilized in schools, where the definition of a well-educated person is more and more narrowly seen in terms of achievement on standardized tests. The studio habits, listed below, were developed to describe the kinds of thinking nurtured by art and necessary to make art, and we have also used them as a framework to inform and transform thinking and knowledge across disciplines beyond art, including the work of learning to teach.

- Develop craft—use and care for tools and materials. Learning artistic conventions.
- Engage and persist—embrace problems of relevance within the art world, of personal importance, or of both to develop focus and other mental states conducive to working and persevering at art tasks.
- Envision—picture mentally what cannot be directly observed and imagine possible next steps in making a piece of art.
- Express—create works that convey an idea, a feeling, or a personal meaning.
- Observe—attend to visual contexts more closely than ordinary "looking" requires, and thereby see things that otherwise might not be seen.
- Reflect: questioning and explaining—think and talk with others about an aspect of one's work or working processes.
- Evaluating—judge one's own work and working processes and the work of others in relation to standards of the field.
- Stretch and explore—reach beyond one's capacities, to explore playfully without a preconceived plan and to embrace the opportunity to learn from mistakes and accidents.
- Understand the art world: domain—art history and current practice.
- Communities—interact as an artist with other artists and within the broader society. (Hetland et al., 2007, p. 6)

As an elementary and middle school art teacher, Arzu Mistry helped foreground her students' thinking and artistic process by making students aware when they were using the above habits of mind. She encouraged a culture of reflection to surface in her classes, thus validating students' methods of working through problems. For example, Arzu used a guided meditation designed so her middle school students could think about their own strengths, challenges, and fears as artists. The class discussed the artists they were currently and the artists they wanted to be. Using two concentric circles, students placed their current selves in the inner circle and used the outer circle to symbolize the artists they wanted to become. The eight studio habits became pathways to get from the inner to the outer circle. For Arzu, the greatest strength of the habits of mind is that students see that skill building, or developing craft, often considered the only important aspect of art making, is just one of eight habits of mind that artists use when they are in the process of making art.

The studio habits can help teachers value the growth of the "whole artist" in the classroom. Students who are highly observant, reflective, or experimental ("stretch and explore") can understand their strengths as artists and not be discouraged because their skill ("develop craft") may not be as high as another student's. This is especially important in elementary school, where students are forming their identities as artists and get easily discouraged when their work does not look as "pretty" as someone else's.

In her work team-teaching with third-grade teachers at ASCEND School, Arzu used student reflections to help make students' thinking visible in an arts-integrated project. She developed simple questions focused on just a few habits of mind in order to help students understand their personal growth as observers. This rich source of ongoing assessment cast new light upon Arzu's observations about students' abilities and process and made visible to students what *they* thought about their own ability and work. Arzu would often quote passages from students' written reflections when she gave them face-to-face feedback. Reading students' reflections gave her a way of responding to their individual needs and informed her planning and classroom practice. The students were writing every day, so Arzu would often read students' reflections aloud to them the next day or use bits and pieces of their reflections in their "starting circle." This consistent feedback, articulation of their growth, and validation of their thoughts increased students' engagement in the reflective process. The students began to look forward to the daily reflections and feedback.

Using the studio habits of mind shifts the focus of arts integration to the mental processes used in making or interpreting art rather than the products typically associated with "tag on art projects" (Tunks & Moseley Grady, 2003) such as posters about *The House on Mango Street* (Cisneros, 1991) or dioramas illustrating daily life in Mayan civilization that come at the end of a curriculum unit and are only loosely connected to learning in art or other disciplines. When such projects are used to promote student understanding rather than only to make a beautiful artifact, teachers are more likely to integrate the arts into a lesson's central purpose rather than add them on at the end. When arts are central to the lesson's purpose, students are more likely to see how thinking in art connects to, furthers, or challenges thinking in the disciplines you teach. Similarly, they see how thinking in other disciplines connects to, furthers, or challenges thinking in art.

For example, a poster project about *The House on Mango Street* might be transformed from product-oriented "tag on" to process-oriented and learning-centered by showing a variety of book covers of *The House on Mango Street* from different editions and various countries (look for images at online booksellers), teaching how to read a visual text and employ artistic techniques used in graphic art, comparing the book's themes as they are highlighted in the covers, and discussing how covers shape an audience's expectations for a book and therefore the meaning they make from reading. Finally, students would create their own covers, employing the techniques they've studied to express their own understanding of the central themes of the novel. As you can see from this example, students' learning in art helps their understanding of *The House on Mango Street*, and their learning in English shapes their knowledge of book covers. And in the process, students learn how artists, writers, and readers think.

As the above example shows, art and disciplines like English, social studies, science, and math are connected in two ways. First, art is about something, and that something, otherwise known as subject matter, often lends itself to deeper understanding. Think about how art is central to your understanding of some historical eras, for example. Second, art is a valuable point of entry for studying various disciplines and fields. Because of these connections between art and subject matter, the studio habits can serve as the conceptual framework for thinking about learning and teaching in English, social studies, science, and math, in addition to art.

Artists often begin their creative thinking by asking a variety of probing questions, and these link closely to various studio habits of mind. All of them link to Understand Art World and Reflect; many emphasize Observe, Envision, and Express; a few specify Engage and Persist and Stretch and Explore. Notably, Develop Craft is often not emphasized at the questioning stage, since developing artistic technique is usually not the purpose of a teacher of an academic subject. The following list, developed by art teacher Todd Elkin, illustrates some of these questions and offers reasons why the questions are a valuable part of teaching with the arts:

> *How can I work through this problem or idea using art?*
> This question pushes students to develop the perseverance of an artist and the discipline required for all rigorous thinking and problem-solving (links to Engage & Persist, Observe, and Envision).

> *How can I use art to show the things I learned about this?*
> Asking this question acknowledges that art not only develops understanding but makes students' learning visible (links to Envision, Observe, and Express).

> *How can I use art to persuade people that my opinion about this is correct?*
> Students remember that art is powerful, provocative, and potentially world-changing when they consider this question (links to Express and Observe).

> *How can I use art to explain this?*
> Students who ask this question understand that art is a way to communicate, illuminate, and develop understanding in others. It can give shape to the world of the viewer (links to Envision and Express).

> *How can I use art to brainstorm new ideas?*
> This question reflects our understanding that art helps us envision what we cannot already see and understand what we do not already know (links to Envision).

How can I use art to show how things are similar or different?
> Art can help us understand by analogy and through metaphor (links to Envision, Observe, and Express).

How can humor, juxtaposition, exaggeration, persuasion, emphasis, and repetition help me explain this to you?
> This question highlights the formal strategies used by artists to make meaning and give shape to their worlds (links to Express and Envision).

How can I use spontaneity, improvisation, and even mistakes to understand this better? (links to Stretch and Explore)
> This question reminds us that learning follows no linear paths, requires intellectual flexibility, and occasionally results in surprises.

Teachers and students can ask the above questions and others like them to get at important habits of mind and curricular understandings. Asking these types of questions is a rich, flexible, and engaging method of taking students and ourselves on targeted quests toward deeper understandings, where artists' thinking processes are a model of meaning-making. The kinds of questions listed above can be utilized before, during, and after planning curriculum. In this manner the thought processes in which artists engage can add depth and resonance to the work you do in your classrooms.

WHERE DO I PLACE THE ARTS IN MY CURRICULUM?

Knowing why you teach generally and why you integrate the arts in particular makes it easier to determine where to place the arts in a course. Are the arts central to your course and part of each unit or lesson? Do the arts constitute separate units or lessons through the year? Do they make an occasional appearance?

Because we see the arts supporting habits of thinking that are part of thinking in other disciplines, we believe they can stand at the center of a course. In introducing their classes to teachers, David and Jen's syllabus says, "We have placed art at the center of our course, because we believe that making and interpreting art requires and develops sophisticated cognitive abilities. Learning the arts is not only about creative expression; it is about thinking, knowledge, and understanding." We reached our rationale after going through a process of reflection on our goals and values. Our rationale for placing arts at the center is similar to those made by educators who place language, particularly reading and writing, at the center of curriculum. Such educators maintain that, as Donmoyer (1995) points out, "all knowing, learning, and thinking is symbolically mediated." He continues, "To this proposition, arts educators only need to add a rather self-evident caveat: language is not the only form of symbolization that figures into learning and thought" (p. 14). We also considered how our course fit into the broader context of our students' entire educational program.

Placing the arts at the center of the curriculum is also a way to compensate for the lack of arts that many students have experienced in public schools, particularly those serving poor students and students of color (Carey, Kleiner, Porch, & Farris, 2002). Consequently, in addition to "releasing the imagination" of students (Greene, 1995), arts integration, in some cases, provides a first-ever exposure to arts. However, integrating arts should never be a substitute for teaching arts as their own subject—rather, it is a curricular enhancement used by non–arts teachers.

Centering a course around the arts fosters the thinking required to develop a philosophy of life, participate in public life, gain access to and succeed in higher education, and prepare for sophisticated jobs characteristic of a knowledge economy. As Eisner (2004) writes, "Academic schooling would do well to look more like the processes the arts celebrate. In the current educational policy climate we have it upside down. The arts are not marginal niceties; they should be regulative ideas for all we do" (p. 8).

Considering where to place the arts in the curriculum raises further questions about how to do so. How do you find the time and other resources for placing arts at the center of a course, unit, or lesson? How can you "start small" and still go beyond placing the arts at the peripheral edges of curriculum?

HOW IMPORTANT IS IT TO MAKE ART?

While not the only component, making art is one of the most crucial ways of integrating the arts. What role will making art play in your curriculum? Do you consider yourself an artist? If so, how can you make your own thinking about learning from making art visible to your students so that they can apprentice in how to learn from making art? If you do not see yourself as an artist, how does your own comfort level influence your thinking about providing opportunities for students to make art? As a check on your thinking, ask whether you consider yourself a reader or a writer. If you do not, do you still include opportunities for students to read or write in your class? We suspect you do, and exploring the reasons for that before you make any decisions about having students make art may help you. Return to your experience in the first section of this chapter, making a symbol to describe arts' importance. That experience can help you see that making art is valuable and that it is not daunting, even as you acknowledge that you have more to learn about making and understanding art.

Developing a symbol was a constructivist process through which you created meaning by bridging new ideas and experiences to prior knowledge and beliefs. According to Fosnot (1996), constructivism is a theory describing knowledge as "temporary, developmental, nonobjective, internally constructed, and socially and culturally mediated" (p. ix). Knowledge is temporary and developmental in the sense that learners are always reconstructing what they know, and their understanding changes as they continue to reflect on the subject of their learning. In pure constructivism, knowledge is nonobjective and internally constructed; it only exists within the persons constructing their learning. No two learners will construct knowledge in exactly the same way. But when we embrace social constructivism, where knowledge is socially and culturally mediated, we connect to the outside world, too; learning does not happen in a vacuum, and what we know as participants in the larger environment shapes how we make sense of new knowledge, connect it to what we already know, and develop schemas for understanding the world.

Because we see learning as a social-constructivist process, making art adds value because making art gives students an authentic experience on which they reflect, before, during, and afterward, to deepen learning. We have found the three studio structures (Hetland et al., 2007) to be helpful in thinking about what making art looks like in our classroom and making the social-constructivist process visible. The three structures are (1) demonstration lectures, where teachers, artists, and others with knowledge about the arts model art making and the thinking processes that accompany them, (2) students-at-work, where students—with varying degrees of teacher involvement—are involved independently or in groups with art making, and (3) critique, where teachers and students observe and reflect on their art and artistic processes.

Making art using these studio structures to guide classroom planning allows diverse students to create new understanding collectively. That understanding includes students developing models of their own thinking, thinking about and visualizing relevant metaphors about the subject, synthesizing information from diverse sources, and developing appreciation for the power of art as a learning tool. In this way, shaping students' attitudes toward the arts in conjunction with making art both enhances learning of the nonart subject and prepares students to be confident and knowledgeable about the arts and how they contribute to learning. Merely being "exposed" to or hearing about the arts does little to spark reflection that leads to understanding. Sadly, many students learn from prior school experiences that they cannot make art or that art is only about making something aesthetically pleasing, not about learning from the process. The process of making art and reflecting on that experience challenges prior assumptions about who is an artist and what artists do and know.

Making art requires us as teachers to stretch and question our own thinking. Teaching is an inherently uncertain profession (McDonald, 1992), and yet teachers still seek certainty. Even teachers who believe that learning is a developmental and social-constructivist process may still believe in one best method of teaching a skill or topic. Such inconsistencies are human and speak to the challenges of our profession. If few things are more uncertain or disequilibrating than learning, doesn't making art only increase frustration and disequilibration? We believe that art making is important precisely because being thrown off center gives students the opportunity to "have wonderful ideas" (Duckworth, 2006), to see that learning is more serendipitous and unpredictable than one might imagine, given the thickness of many textbooks full of facts. These wonderful ideas become more possible when students make their thinking visible to themselves and others, something nurtured by making art.

Arts integration takes time and, like all teachers integrating the arts, we have struggled with time limitations in our own work. Given all that we feel responsible for teaching, we sometimes wonder whether we can devote class time to drawing or making collages or accordion books. But art making can be fast and informal. For example, when David and Jen wanted to introduce the studio habits of mind, we asked students to make two quick contour drawings of a chair—one blind (looking only at the object they are drawing, not the paper on which they are drawing it) and one sighted (looking at both object and paper). A contour drawing requires students to draw what they see without taking their pencil off the paper. After both drawings, we asked students to compare their work and reflect on the thinking in which they were engaged while making the drawings. In this activity, students uncovered for themselves many of the studio habits of mind. In particular, they came to understand more deeply what it means to observe and then connected this to the arts and other subject-matter goals for their curriculum.

As the final reflection on the contour drawing illustrates, looking at art engages many of the same habits of mind as making art, and artists have their own way of "reading" art. If your students do not make art, they can still engage in studio habits like observation by slowing down to find meaning in a work and carefully noting multiple dimensions of a work of visual, performed, or literary art, or of science, mathematics, or history. They can reflect on the connection of a work—of art or in another discipline—to their lives, to other works, and to the world. They can understand the art world (or the mathematics, history, literary, or science worlds) as they place work in historical and aesthetic contexts.

Finally, while you will generally experience appreciation and a desire to learn more about and through the arts from most students, we acknowledge that arts integration can also meet with resistance. Some resist because they do not see the immediate relevance of the arts to learning. With these students, ask yourself how you can broaden students' perspectives on what it means to understand subject matter. Others resist because they think of school as restrictive and irrelevant, so something authentic feels out of place. This raises for us the importance of using arts integration as a means to change students' attitudes toward school and as a motivator for learning. Still other students resist because they see the arts as elitist and contrary to other valued goals like equity and social justice. Consider ways to show these students that artists and the arts have a long tradition of giving voice and identity to those on the margins of power, speaking out against injustice, and presenting alternative perspectives and imagining a better future.

Reflecting on the importance of making art raises questions about what "art" is. Do all student "products" qualify? And is all art equally appropriate to arts integration? Do some art forms lend themselves more readily than others? How might those decisions about most appropriate art forms vary depending on the disciplines with which art is being integrated?

HOW MUCH OF AN ARTIST DO I NEED TO BE?

Right now you might be thinking: "How can I integrate the arts? I can't even draw!" Or "I can't dance to save my life!" But instead of giving up on integrating the arts, you can gain more confidence about your knowledge of art by making art in a context where the emphasis is not on technical perfection but on learning from the process of making art. For that reason, we encourage you to ensure that making art is part of any professional development on arts integration. Ask your principal or coordinator of professional development to bring in teaching artists who can teach you and other colleagues about art and how to learn from the experience through making art. For example, Guitars in the Classroom (www.guitarsintheclassroom.org) is a professional development program that prepares teachers, even those with no musical experience, to play the guitar in 8 weeks. It also provides free guitars to students so teachers can integrate music in their classrooms. Teachers do not have to be artists to integrate the arts. If you are worried that you are not enough of an expert to integrate the arts on your own, you need only be ready to collaborate with others who are.

You can also gain more confidence about arts integration by redefining what art is and what artists do. For example, much contemporary visual art illustrates that artists do not have to draw. And modern dance focuses on movement and expression rather than perfect rendering of movements such as in classical ballet. Rather than focusing on technical skills in a particular art medium, you can start to focus on the studio habits of mind—that is, on how artists think.

And to those of you who are experts at one or more forms of art, we are glad you are in the classroom. We also caution you to make sure that the thinking behind your expertise is not invisible to students. Experts can make the arts look "easy" when in fact students learning in and through the arts may need to know how to persist through struggle. Experts can demystify art by sharing how they think about the decisions they make in the process, and the connections they make between their art and all their other knowledge.

The question headlining this section applies not only to you but to your students as well. How expert in art should students be at the end of an arts-integrated lesson in science, history, literature, or mathematics? Although students need not be experts, they should learn something about art as well as the other discipline with which it is integrated. Too often in arts-integrated lessons, students learn new content in history or science, but the art component of the lesson only asks them to draw on what they already know (or do not know) about art to complete an assignment like making a mandala or illustrating a book cover. The equivalent in language arts would be to ask students to write without ever giving them instruction in how to develop their craft or expecting them to grow as writers. Again, collaborating with teaching artists and arts organizations can contribute to your students' arts knowledge and skills.

As you rethink what it means to be an artist, ask yourself these other questions: When collaborating with artists, what am I looking for as an end-in-view of such collaboration? How do I facilitate conversations with artists to connect their work to subject matter in schools? How do my students and I reflect on making art to learn from the experience?

WHAT DOES COLLABORATION LOOK LIKE?

No teacher possesses all the knowledge he or she needs and all teachers possess knowledge worth sharing. Given such a conception of funds of knowledge (González, Moll, & Amanti, 2005), teachers should expect to collaborate.

What might this collaboration look like? We can offer a few insights from our own experience teaching a curriculum course to future teachers. Neither of us began the course with all the knowledge we needed by ourselves to prepare English, social studies, and art teachers, but over time we came to learn from each other. David's experience was in social studies and English–language arts education. Jennifer's was in arts education. Over time, we each learned to understand the language and vocabulary of the other. We asked questions. We got clear about our individual and collaborative goals. Interestingly, at a time when future teachers are encouraged to collaborate, institutional reward structures in higher education that privilege individual accomplishments mean they see few examples. We had to educate others in the institution about the value of collaboration.

In addition to collaborating with each other, we worked with artists and arts institutions in the community. During the course of the year, we worked with local artists and arts educators who share their thinking about making art and incorporating it in their teaching. We have brought teachers to museums to learn about art and to learn about how to use museums in their own curriculum. We have gone on mural walking tours near campus, using the art in the community as a text from which to brainstorm generative topics for curriculum. Based on our own experience, we would encourage teachers not to focus on what they do not know but on what they can learn by working with others.

How do teachers and artists negotiate issues of power and logistics? Should artists become part of the school staff or be hired as freelancers from the community? These are questions you should consider, especially as you make plans at the schoolwide level for arts integration.

WHY THE QUESTIONS MATTER

We know that in answering our own questions, we run the risk of looking like we are making prescriptions for others. We know that other teachers work in contexts and with students different from our own. We have shared our own thinking to spark yours, not to supplant it. We raised further questions at the end of reflecting on each of the five questions to indicate that good questions lead to more questions, not easy answers. Particularly during these times, we see arts integration as a perfect means for raising questions to develop critical thinking, expand perspectives, foster imagination, and bring the student into the classroom by building on existing knowledge and values. It would be ironic, therefore, to think that integrating the arts answered all our questions. Rather, it has raised new questions and new dimensions of old ones. We believe the arts can serve a similar purpose of raising fundamental questions about learning across the disciplines and grade levels.

HOW TO USE THIS BOOK

Artful Teaching is designed to speak to teachers in grades K–8 who are responsible for teaching a variety of subject matter. It does not provide recipes for introducing a particular art form at a particular grade level. Such a book would need dozens of chapters to address multiple art forms for a variety of subject matter at nine different grade levels. Instead, it offers practical examples of teachers integrating the arts at the elementary and middle school levels so you can come away with a deeper understanding of the following:

- Why and how to use the arts to reach *every child*, not only those who are gifted or considered "artistic."
- Why and how the arts can be used in *every school*, not only those with high test scores or wealthy parents.
- Why and how the arts can be used *every day*, not as an add-on but as an integral part of learning important, standards-based disciplinary content.

Because thinking about teaching and how to integrate the arts is not a linear process, you do not have to read this book from start to finish to benefit your practice or push your thinking. You may find it helpful to pick out the chapters that are most relevant to you. Some chapters may be more relevant because of the kind of art being integrated, the subject matter with which art is being integrated, or the grade level of the students being taught. Do not make a narrow decision about what might be relevant, however. We encourage you to skim all the chapters. Even though you may be wondering about integrating music into middle school social studies, you might find something valuable in the questions posed by an author discussing the visual arts in first-grade English-language arts. The authors have framed the chapters so you will find the ideas generative even if your own context is different. All of the contributors are part of the Alliance for Arts Learning Leadership (Alliance for ALL), a Bay Area network of districts and institutions, school leaders and teachers, artists and community members working to promote the role of the arts in a high-quality education, or the Arts Education Initiative, a consortium of Bay Area teacher and leadership educators committed to arts integration in schools and teacher preparation. Because they are drawing from experience teaching and learning in diverse Bay Area settings, we believe the examples and ideas in each chapter will speak to a wide audience of teachers, artists, administrators, and teacher educators.

OUTLINE OF CONTENT AND CHAPTER DESCRIPTIONS

The content is organized in four sections. The first addresses two foundational essential questions about arts and arts integration: 1) What is art? 2) And how are the arts connected to human rights and social justice?

These two opening chapters introduce big ideas and vital conversations that are taking place in the arts today. In asking you to think about "What is art?" for example, the author introduces developments in defining art in the 21st century that have implications for teaching across grade levels and subject matter. Connecting the arts to human rights and social justice addresses why we teach generally and is an important rationale for why we integrate the arts specifically in our curriculum.

The following three parts are organized according to the mission of the Alliance for Arts Learning Leadership (Alliance for ALL): Art for every child in every school every day. The Alliance for ALL has played a leading role in the Bay Area in bringing multiple constituencies together to support arts learning and arts integration. Its motto speaks to the goal of providing all children with meaningful arts learning so that they can become creative and critical thinkers, effective communicators, responsible citizens, and knowledgeable adults. Each aspect of ALL's motto corresponds to a section in *Artful Teaching* and the goals of each chapter.

In the section "Art for Every Child," the chapter authors explore what it means to teach all children well using the arts, including how the arts contribute to teaching the whole child, how art is an entry point and motivator for learning, how the arts develop content-area understanding and thinking skills across disciplines and grade levels, and how the arts make all children's learning visible. These chapters describe how providing the arts to all children is an issue of equity; they address how teachers and administrators can find allies and collaborate with others to bring the arts to all children.

In the section "Art in Every School," the contributors look at how school leaders, teachers, and teaching artists build a culture to support arts learning at the school level, including through professional development. In this section, equity is addressed by looking at arts integration across diverse school contexts. School leaders interested in creating a schoolwide culture supporting arts integration will find inspiration and specific ideas in these chapters.

In the "Art Every Day" section, the authors examine how the arts connect home and school; promote equitable access to important subject matter; and build community among students, teachers, and parents. This section provides examples of integrating the arts in a variety of subject areas and how to collaborate with teaching artists. While the authors share details about specific lessons, experiences, and examples of student work, these examples can serve as starting points for thinking about the possibilities of arts integration in your own practice. The final chapter in this section describes how to find teaching artist partners to make the arts part of lessons every day across the curriculum.

In addition to teachers, both teacher educators and professional development leaders should find this section useful for thinking about how to incorporate the arts into their own practice and how to prepare future teachers to integrate the arts in theirs. Artists and teaching artists working with K–8 classroom teachers should also benefit from this section by thinking about how to use their knowledge and skills best to support children's learning in the arts and other academic disciplines.

REFERENCES

Bains, R., & Mesa-Bains, A. (2002). A reciprocal university: A model for arts, justice, and community. *Social Justice, 29*(4), 182–197.

Blythe, T. (1997). *The teaching for understanding guide.* San Francisco: Jossey-Bass.

Carey, N., Kleiner, B., Porch, R., & Farris, E. (2002). *Arts education in public elementary and secondary schools: 1999–2000.* (NCES 2002131). U.S. Department of Education. Washington, DC: NCES.

Cisneros, S. (1991). *The House on Mango Street.* New York: Vintage.

Cochran-Smith, M. (1991). Learning to teach against the grain. *Harvard Educational Review, 61*(3), 279–310.

Donahue, D. (2005). Preparing and supporting the reflective practitioner. In Kroll, L., et al., *Teaching as principled practice: Managing complexity for social justice* (pp. 35–56). Thousand Oaks, CA: Sage.

Donmoyer, R. (1995). The arts as modes of learning and methods of teaching: A (borrowed and adapted) case for integrating the arts across the curriculum. *Arts Education Policy Review, 96*(5), 14–20.

Duckworth, E. (2006). *"The having of wonderful ideas" and other essays on teaching and learning.* New York: Teachers College Press.

Efland, A. (2002). *Art and cognition: Integrating the visual arts in the curriculum.* New York: Teachers College Press.

Eisner, E. (2002). *Arts and the creation of mind.* New Haven, CT: Yale University Press.

Eisner, E. (2004, October). *What the arts contribute to a child's development.* Keynote address, California Educational Theater Association Conference.

Fiske, E. (Ed.). (1999). *Champions of change: The impact of the arts on learning*. Washington, DC: Arts Education Partnership and Presidents' Committee on the Arts and Humanities.

Fosnot, C. (1996). *Constructivism: Theory, perspectives, and practice*. New York: Teachers College Press.

Fowler, C. (1996). *Strong arts, strong schools: The promising potential and shortsighted disregard of the arts in American schooling*. New York: Oxford University Press.

Gardner, H. (1993). *Frames of mind: The theory of multiple intelligences*. New York: Basic Books.

Gay, G., & Kirkland, K. (2003). Developing cultural critical consciousness and self-reflection in preservice teacher education. *Theory into Practice, 43*(3), 181–187.

González, N., Moll, L., & Amanti, C. (2005). *Funds of knowledge: Theorizing practices in households, communities, and classrooms*. Mahwah, NJ: Lawrence Erlbaum Associates.

Greene, M. (1995). *Releasing the imagination: Essays on education, arts, and social change*. San Francisco: Jossey-Bass.

Heck, M. (2001). Eye messages: A partnership of artmaking and multicultural education. *Multicultural Perspectives, 3*(1), 3–8.

Hetland, L., & Winner, E. (2001). The arts and academic achievement: What the evidence shows. *Arts Education Policy Review, 102*(5), 3–6.

Hetland, L., Winner, E., Veenema, S., & Sheridan, K. (2007). *Studio thinking: The real benefits of visual arts education*. New York: Teachers College Press.

Hoffman Davis, J. (2008). *Why our schools need the arts*. New York: Teachers College Press.

Lowenfeld, V. (1947). *Creative and mental growth*. New York: Macmillan.

Mbuyamba, L. (2006, March). *Report on the closing session of the UNESCO world conference on arts education: Building creative capacities for the 21st century, Lisbon, Portugal*. Paris: United Nations Educational, Scientific, and Cultural Organisation.

McDonald, J. (1992). *Teaching: Making sense of an uncertain craft*. New York: Teachers College Press.

Perkins, D. (1994). *The intelligent eye: Learning to think by looking at art*. Los Angeles: J. Paul Getty Trust.

Rabkin, N. (2004). Introduction: Learning and the arts. In N. Rabkin & R. Redmond (Eds.), *Putting the arts in the picture: Reframing education in the 21st century* (pp. 5–13). Chicago: Columbia College Chicago.

Stevenson, L. M., & Deasy, R. J. (2005). *Third space: When learning matters*. Washington, DC: Arts Education Partnership.

Tunks, J., & Moseley Grady, P. (2003). Arts infusion in university courses: The effect on student choice to infuse art in elementary classes. *Curriculum and Teaching Dialogue, 5*(1), 61–70.

Tyack, D., & Cuban, L. (1997). *Tinkering toward utopia*. Cambridge, MA: Harvard University Press.

PART I

Essential Questions About the Arts and Integration

CHAPTER 1

What Is Art?

Laurie Polster

Art is creation, imagination, recording, investigation, arbitration, and culmination. It helps define our existence and makes us less alone and frees our frustrations. Of course art matters.
—Anonymous, Yale Art Gallery, *What Is Art and Why Does It Matter?*

ART IS AN essential form of expression and communication, an expansive and diverse language fundamentally connected to experiencing and engaging in the world around us. As we begin to explore the possibilities for arts integration, let's start at the beginning: What is art? As we consider this question, a number of related questions emerge, including whether art has to be made in a certain way, whether it needs to be exhibited or presented in a museum or theater, and what shapes our perception of art at any given time.

When you think about "art," what is the first thing that comes to mind? Most of us think of art as an *object*, a physical manifestation of creative expression. We generally think of something tangible, for example a drawing, painting, or sculpture, or something performed or viewed that can often be replicated, like a song, play, film, or dance. We're probably aware that the work of art was constructed in some deliberate fashion—not just physically, but visually, aurally, temporally, culturally, and conceptually. Works of art rely on and incorporate multiple layers of sensory language as well as historical and cultural information.

But we may not be cognizant of the underlying thinking in which artists engage when creating works of art, or have much understanding of how that thinking relates to how we construct the meaning of any given work of art. To integrate the arts successfully in our teaching, we need to develop a broader understanding of *what art is*, as well as a deeper understanding of the related thinking that goes into its creation. With this knowledge we can then begin to shape ways to incorporate artistic processes into our own teaching in a resonant and relevant approach that engages and challenges our students as well as ourselves.

So, what *is* art? While teaching at an elementary school, I heard that a group of colleagues had a challenging discussion about what constitutes authentic art-making in their classrooms, and what types of integrated arts projects would be creatively valuable for their students. One teacher apparently asked about making dioramas, to which another adamantly responded, "A diorama is *not* art!" How I wished I had been present to engage that discussion further. At that very moment, not 25 miles from our school, the Bedford Gallery, a major art center in Walnut Creek, California, was presenting *The Art of Diorama*, an exhibition that examined the form made popular in mid-19th-century Britain and France. The exhibit brought dioramas up to the 21st century and included works by a number of contemporary American artists who, using sculpture, painting, video, and photography, had constructed "life-like environments or habitats blending real and imagined elements to capture a single and arrested moment in time" (Bedford Gallery, 2009).

What made these dioramas "art"? The curator of exhibitions, Carrie Lederer, related that many of the artists, when asked why they worked in diorama, spoke of "being captured by dioramas at an early age, the allure coming from a cherished doll house, a prized train set, trips with mom and dad to the natural history museum" (KQED Arts, 2009). Some artists' work played with the perception of what is expected, while others created ideas that explore where we have come from and where we are going or used materials in unexpected ways.

One Bay Area diorama artist, Tracy Snelling, builds small-scale installations and sculptures of buildings and landscapes. Snelling is interested in representing places in extreme detail—letting stories unfold as the viewer encounters a space in which the lives of the inhabitants (not present) play out in the artist's choice of objects, lighting, and composition. For example, in one room of one building in the diorama, you might see on a television an old movie and hear the sound of soulful music playing in the background. If we look at Snelling's example, we see the enormous possibilities of taking a recognizable and seemingly fixed form, in this case diorama, and expanding our concept of that framework beyond "shoebox projects" from our childhood, using it as a springboard for unlimited creative expression. Using this as a paradigm, how else might we broaden and challenge our expectations and assumptions concerning *what is art*?

ART MAKING: WHAT'S IT ALL ABOUT?

"looking for ways to bottle the lightning"
                                        —A. Kahn, *Mick Jagger: A Stone Alone*

At its core, art is creative expression, and art making is the *process* of that expression—the inquiry and engagement, research and experimentation, trial

Figure 1.1. *Chongqing,* Diorama by Tracy Snelling.

and error, risk-taking, reflection and reevaluation, and growth and discovery. Art can be both evocative and provocative, evoking all types of sensations, emotions, and states of awareness from ecstasy to despair, and provoking intellectual inquiry, alternative understanding and consciousness, as well as personal, social, and political action. Art is about interpreting and reinterpreting ideas, exploring and developing multiple avenues of sensory communication and language forms. It's about discovering and developing one's personal voice and making that voice public, through sharing the artwork with a larger community, be it the person sitting next to you or the world at large.

Creating art provides a forum to delve into ideas and material that might not readily be expressed through verbal discourse alone, or whose meaning may be expanded through artistic presentation. An important role of art is to make the marginal central, to give purpose and voice to that which seems off balance. At the same time, making art provides an enormously valuable space for not yet discovered, unarticulated, or nonverbal ideas to bubble forth into consciousness and take shape in a life of their own—be they drawn, printed, spoken, sung, performed, exhibited, recorded, or documented and digitally transmitted. It is through such creative processes that we discover and reflect outward some aspects of ourselves, our community, and our relationship to the world. As the vocalist/musician Lipbone Redding (2007) noted, "If it's alive, then it's art"—you can feel it, touch it, taste it, see it, hear it, breathe it.

Given this expansive definition of art, what will art making in your classroom be about? How might you help kindergarten students learn to interpret and reinterpret art and other texts? How might you encourage middle school students to find a voice and make it public?

MATERIALS AND PROCESS: IS ART MADE IN A SPECIFIC WAY?

"The brain is a category buster," according to the cognitive neuroscientist Elizabeth Phelps (Lehrer, 2007), and that single statement translates directly to creative processes. Art can encompass just about anything, and that includes the materials that go into the creation of the work, as well as the approach an individual artist or collaborative team takes in creating work. Writing about Joseph Cornell, an acclaimed self-taught artist who worked almost exclusively with found materials to create boxes, collages, and films, Lynda Roscoe Hartigan, in a text accompanying a 2007 exhibition at the San Francisco Museum of Modern Art, describes creative processes that are true for academically trained artists as well: "Making something new from preexisting materials is critical to the process of many self-taught artists. It is also central to the modern concept of creativity as the collision and recombination of ideas. As a result traditions can be reinterpreted, and connections can be forged between the seemingly random and disparate."

By itself, a ball is a rather mundane object, something most often used in sports. It could easily stand in as a visual symbol for a basketball game or a symbolic metaphor for a globe, but it could just as readily become the percussion instrument for a live or recorded spoken word or musical performance. In other words, a ball, in the mind and hands of an artist, is not just *a ball*.

For example, composer Steven Mackey (2008), "fascinated by the one-man band mentality of juggling contrasting timbres produced by a gamut ranging from finely crafted instruments to kitchen utensils," included in his scored percussion the sight and sound of a fluorescent green tennis ball dropped and bounced to rest on a bass drum. In a vastly different rendering, composer Maggi Payne transformed layered sounds composed of processed close-up recordings of ball bearings bouncing on dry ice into frantic "windstorms" stirring up a vast frozen expanse in her composition *Arctic Winds* (2007). Also influenced by nature, Bay Area artist Carrie Leeb draws inspiration from ball rock formations in deserts like California's Anza Borrego and Chile's Atacama to create sculptures from lint that convey a sense of calmness, slowness, and quiet.

The artist Andy Goldsworthy (2001) released 13 giant snowballs measuring 6–7 feet on the streets of the city of London on the summer solstice in June 2000— "an astonishingly powerful piece of work . . . [and] a huge attention grabber to the fact that climate change is having very real impacts on peoples' lives all over the planet" (Greenpeace, 2000). He donated the proceeds from photographs to

Figure 1.2. Untitled No. 3, Carrie Leeb, 2009, lint and thread.

benefit Greenpeace, an example of the arts supporting social and political issues. One of the snowballs, made from Scottish winter snow, kept in cold storage and transferred to London for the exhibition, ended up outside British Petroleum's headquarters, highlighting the role that oil companies play in the meltdown affecting the Arctic ice cap.

So, if a ball can become more than just a ball, in what other ways might materials be used to construct meaning and reveal something unexpected? Recycled and salvaged materials—be they newspapers, cardboard tubes, aluminum cans, plastic containers, packing materials, wire, buttons, clothing, furniture, advertisements, or sound-source material—are readily available and adaptable for all types of projects. Taking students on a walk through their neighborhood to pick up cast-offs, trash, and recyclables can be an ecological and sociological eye-opener as well as a treasure hunt. Incorporating and transforming that detritus into something else—beautiful, funny, humorous, practical, absurd, disturbing—can become a creative adventure as well as a vehicle for ecological and social comment. If we nurture and value the process of art making, how might we challenge our students to utilize materials beyond their intended function, and in so doing explore conceptual linkages within their own lives and in their surrounding environment?

WHAT AFFECTS OUR PERCEPTION OF ART?

We don't see things as they are, we see them as we are.
—Anaïs Nin, in R. Epstein, "Mindful Practice"

Think how important and integral rests or breaks are in a musical composition, a monologue, a dance, or a film. We don't actually understand voice or sound except in relation to the silence around it. Meaning is created in the breath or space of absence, the negative spaces. We perceive something through its relationship and juxtaposition to its surrounding elements, whether these be concrete objects or ideas. As we attempt to give meaning to the whole, our understanding shifts in relation to how we view the sum of various parts, yet we are not always aware of what those parts encompass or what parts may be missing from the picture as a whole.

If we look at color, there's a layer to our response beyond the physiological perception of retinal/brain decoding. Myriad cultural and psychological factors affect how we perceive color. For instance, red is a primary color, one of the three main colors from which you can make all other colors with pigments. On the spectrum it is considered a warm color. Warm colors often remind us of the sun and fire; the cool colors are greens, blues, and purples, which might remind us of water, summer leaves, or daytime sky. How we see color and respond to it depends on the relationship to its surroundings, including the other colors around it, as well as how it is lit, in addition to our emotional response to it. This last response is by no means universal. While red can appear energetic and festive to some, it could well appear fiery, gaudy, or frightening to others, depending both on how it is used and on how it is perceived.

If we examine the work of the Mexican artists Frida Kahlo and Diego Rivera, we notice that the palette is often vibrant and lush, relying on a strong use of reds that are often juxtaposed with green (Souter, 2007). The use of color in Latin American art reflects the culture where the work was made; if you travel to Mexico or Guatemala, you see similar colors and color combinations present in everything from textiles and street signage to furniture, painting, and sculpture. Until more recently, art historians trained in European sensibilities of how to use color considered much of this Latin American artwork overly colorful and even garish. What does this say about the perception of color and cultural values—and if so, how might experiencing art broaden our perceptual and cultural understanding?

In a similar vein, our appreciation of music is linked to exposure and familiarity, in addition to personal interest. Middle Eastern and Indian music contain modes (scales and forms) with microtonal intervals, intervals of less than half a note apart, that are not found in Western musical scales. To the uninitiated, these unfamiliar scales and intervals can seem awkward and strange, and even be perceived as disorienting and "incorrect," with notes sounding flat or sharp as if the performer were playing or singing out of tune. Instruments from around the world produce a variety of pitches and timbres and are used to different effect in various arrangements, combinations, and types of music, specific to culture and genre. What may be considered pleasant sounding and natural to someone who has spent a lifetime listening to Chinese classical music may be very different from what someone only familiar with Western musical styles and instrumentation considers pleasing. Likewise, hearing a saxophone arrangement of Johann Sebastian Bach's classical repertoire performed in a symphonic concert hall might seem equally challenging or inspiring to some listeners. In these contexts, value judgments may be unknowingly and inadvertently placed on both the quality of the music as well as the ability of the performer.

Receptivity to various arts is also shaped by communal and state support (or lack thereof) for those arts. Historically, numerous art forms have been categorically encouraged, ignored, sanctioned, suppressed, or denigrated for a variety of sociopolitical reasons affecting how the work is valued, labeled, and received. Interestingly, some art forms—for example, tango (arising from the barrios of Buenos Aires, Argentina) and hip-hop—have emerged in spite of social denigration, and partially because of it, to reach global acceptance and success.

Are there other implications of labeling in regards to perceptual understanding? When the sculptor Martin Puryear was asked about the genesis of *Ladder for Booker T. Washington*, his 36-foot suspended-ladder piece, he responded: "The title came after the work was finished. . . . I didn't set out to make a work about Booker T. Washington. The title was very much a second stage in the whole evolution of the work" (*Art 21*, 2003). For Puryear, the sculpture was about using the sapling, the tree itself, and making a work that had a kind of artificial, forced, and exaggerated perspective that made it appear to recede into space. When looking at the tip, the viewer is clearly aware that it is not as far away as the artist is telling you, the diminished perspective created by a device first used extensively in the Renaissance. But another key aspect of the work is its reference to ladders, literally, since it *is* a ladder, made like a country ladder from a split sapling with rungs.

What is the connection between what's going on in the work and the title of the piece? Puryear believes that the piece is about perspective. "And the idea of Booker T. Washington, the resonance with his life, and his struggle . . . the whole notion that his idea of progress for the race was a long slow, gradual progression of, as he said, 'Putting your buckets down where you are and working with what you've got.'" The artist contrasts Washington's perspective with W. E. B. Du Bois, "who was a much more radical thinker and who had a much more pro-active way of thinking about racial struggle for equality." For Puryear, the work raises "the whole notion of where you start and where you want to get to and how far away it really is. And if it's possible to get there given the circumstances that you're operating within. The joining of that idea of Booker T. Washington and his notion of progress and the form of that piece—that came after the fact. But when I thought about a title for it, it just seemed absolutely fitting" (*Art 21*, 2003).

So what does this tell us about what influences perception? Since perception is shaped by our experience and awareness, do the arts in your classroom broaden the range of students' perspectives and cultural understanding? How can you integrate art to provide multiple perspectives and deepen students' understanding of art and its cultural and historical contexts?

CAN THE MEANING OF A WORK OF ART CHANGE?

Sometimes doing something poetic can become political, and sometimes doing something political can become poetic.
    —F. Alÿs, *Sometimes Doing Something Poetic Can Become Political and Sometimes Doing Something Political Can Become Poetic*

The impact of a specific work of art can change dramatically when the context in which it is presented is altered. Although the actual work remains the same, the experience of seeing or hearing it may be radically different given varying contexts. An example is the civil rights movement song "We Shall Overcome," made famous by the legendary folk singer Pete Seeger.

Seeger initially learned the song from a White woman, Zilphia Horton, who taught in a union labor school, the Highlander Folk School, in Tennessee. Tobacco workers were said to have made up the song in 1946 to sing while on strike that winter in Charleston, South Carolina. Horton published it in 1947 in a small New York magazine, *People's Songs*, under the title "We Will Overcome" (*Democracy Now*, 2006).

The song's history goes back even earlier, however. According to a 1909 letter writer in the *United Mine Workers Journal*, "Last year at a strike we opened every meeting with a prayer, and singing that good old song, 'We Will Overcome,'" which places the song probably as a late 19th-century union version of a well-known gospel song, "I'll Overcome, I'll Overcome, I'll Overcome Some Day." Seeger changed the lyrics to "shall" because he thought it sounded better vocally (*Democracy Now*, 2006).

In 1957, Seeger performed the song during the Highlander School's 25th anniversary celebration, where Dr. Martin Luther King Jr. and Reverend Ralph Abernathy were also participating. The song stuck with Dr. King, but he was not a song leader. So it was not until 3 years later, in 1960, that a friend of Seeger's, Guy Carawan, taught it to the young people at the founding convention of the Student Non-Violent Coordinating Committee (SNCC). A month later, it wasn't just *a* song, it was *the* song, throughout the civil rights movement of the South (*Democracy Now*, 2006).

Seeger always said that the beauty of a song is in how it can be used and reused and changed for different purposes. "We Shall Overcome" was used in the civil rights movement and later in the freedom movement Tiananmen Square and in many other movements around the world. When Jim Musselman put out the first volume of *The Songs of Pete Seeger*, it included a newly revised Bruce Springsteen rendition of "We Shall Overcome." Initially, the two musicians were criticized for the way Springsteen had personalized the song as if singing to an individual. But then came letters from parents whose children had leukemia, who were singing Springsteen's version to their child, inspiring hope that they would overcome this disease. After the Columbine massacre, Springsteen played the song at one of the funerals, and then after September 11, 2001, NBC News used that rendition as the soundtrack accompanying a video montage of the rescue workers. The video played hourly, the song giving a sense of hope and comfort to people, not only because of Springsteen's voice, but also because the song was familiar and had been used throughout history to overcome so much adversity (*Democracy Now*, 2006).

"We Shall Overcome" is an example of how form and context shape a work of art, and how the work, in turn, affects the surrounding situation. Hearing that fairly simple straightforward song, we are also hearing its roots as a gospel song, a strike song, and a famous civil rights movement song; it continues to be powerful today. The embedded history is carried within the song, even when that history is not fully evident. By revealing it, our connection to the art becomes deeper still. As teachers, how are we helping our students understand the multifaceted history and context of art we incorporate into our curriculum?

WHO DECIDES WHAT ART IS—AND HOW?

Whether to consider a given genre or an individual work as *Art* (with a capital A) is the fodder of ongoing discussion, the controversy being whether a specific creative expression should be included on the pedestal of "highbrow" art—that is, the type of work traditionally seen in museums and galleries—or relegated to the more marginalized category of street art or popular culture. For many years, museums and galleries have been showing a marked interest in the latter category of work, not that this should necessarily affect what we consider *art*. The more important questions are, rather, *who* gets to determine what qualifies as art, and *by what standards* something is judged and ultimately deemed valid, or validated in "official" circles, as creative expression worthy of the label *art*. Ultimately, whether something is defined as art is less important than the conversation about it.

Consider graffiti. Our notion of graffiti depends on what we deem licit and illicit, and meaningful and meaningless, in a wide range of human activities. People have been marking up walls since before written history, but it has only been in recent centuries that they have begun to examine and record the unofficial and prohibited markings we now call graffiti. When Pompeii was excavated in the 18th century from the volcanic ash that had preserved it, its walls were covered with an intact record of scratched and chalked personal odes, vulgar jokes, and social criticisms. It took nearly a century for anyone to study and publish the scribblings as a phenomenon worth noting, giving them the name *graffiti*. As described at one museum exhibit:

> Virtually at the same time that archeologists began to classify graffiti, other writers began to speculate on the connections between such untutored markings and the fundamentals of high art. In the past hundred years, sociologists, psychologists and (much more recently) artists have given close attention to inscriptions of the walls of prisons, latrines, subways, and other public places, as uniquely valuable evidence of individual and social energies, both creative and destructive. (*High and Low*, 1990)

What's important to realize here is that graffiti is not a single phenomenon wedded only to contemporary urban youth, but instead the product of a broad array of individuals and cultures, from the past reflecting into the present.

Another popular genre that fits into this mold is the graphic novel, with roots tracing back as far as cave paintings (also an antecedent to graffiti), and directly connected to comic books. Artist/writers such as Harvey Pekar *(American Splendor)*, Joe Sacco *(Palestine)*, Marjane Satrapi *(Persepolis)*, and Art Spiegelman *(Maus)* have propelled graphic novels into the realm of serious fiction, but not without some major reevaluation of what constitutes respected literature. Given that, how might a discussion of what we name and value as art add to your students' understanding of the world?

WHAT IS OUR STUDENTS' EXPERIENCE WITH ART?

On a daily basis, our students absorb a large dose of rapid-fire visual and verbal messages—some quite creatively designed and packaged—from television, Internet, cell phones, video games, film, music performance, MTV, radio, magazines, and billboards. Their experience of creative expression and representation is in large part shaped by their everyday world, far outside mainstream museum walls or theatrical and performance venues. How we actually process this material—visually, aurally, temporally, and conceptually—and the ability to deconstruct its meaning depend on our awareness of the creative elements and content in play. Furthermore, the ability to utilize this knowledge through open-ended creative explorations that generate further ideas and connections relies on an unrestricted notion of what art is. Our students are already making art, using cell phones, creating impromptu videos and placing them on YouTube, making graffiti and comic strips, using found objects to make sound and street art, creating impromptu movements and replicating dance moves from MTV. Educators recognize the importance of building on students' prior knowledge and experiences (Vygotsky, 1978). This is just as important in art as it is in other subject areas.

Knowing that our students experience and make art broaches interesting questions for us as educators. What is our current notion of art, and is it fully inclusive and expansive, or have we narrowed the horizon, whether consciously or unconsciously, in ways that exclude key issues and modalities surrounding creative expression? To put it simply, how do projects such as community-based collaborative performances, eco-gardens, Web-based multimedia storytelling, guerrilla street theater protests, graphic novels, zines, spoken-word slams, or graffiti fit into our notion of art? And if we do manage to find a comfortable place for them, how on earth do we begin to unpack this material? How do we incorporate any of these artistic processes in our teaching? Given these concerns, what messages, whether explicit or implicit, will your arts-integrated curriculum send to students? For instance, if students are learning about ways to reduce their carbon footprint—turning out lights, eating less meat, bicycling and recycling more—how might you tap into their rich media experience as a launch pad to create infomercials targeting these ideas?

WHO ARE THE ART MAKERS?

This is the moment freedom begins—the moment you realize that some-one else is writing your story and you take the pen from his hand and start writing it yourself.
> —Bill Moyers, on *Democracy Now*, January 16, 2007

We are all artists. Each one of us has something to express, and whether or how we choose to express this creatively is part of a journey. The label of *painter, writer, dancer,* or *musician* may apply to some more than others, but it doesn't encompass the full breadth of creative work done today, nor the individuals who are currently engaged in creative processes. Collectively, artists are reshaping, reclaiming, and reframing stories, both personal and communal, along with the information those stories may be built around, and taking an active, and in many cases inventive, role in transmitting their versions of stories. Who gets to tell the story, and through which art form, is in the hands of each and every one of us.

Art comes in all shapes, sizes, and dimensions, and it by no means starts or ends with a product. There are mail art projects, where work gets traded, altered, and shipped to the next participant in an ongoing process. A more recent techno-logically driven version of this uses the Internet to share and communally develop art. There are personal journals and public blogs; murals and temporary installa-tion projects; dance, music, and poetry slams.

The following rap, collaged from appropriated quotations, sums up several of the big ideas we have examined in this chapter. Use it as a launch pad for further exploration.

> Art is confusing. It keeps us awake
> It's what people care about—what they love and hate
> Art is the impractical aspect of everything
> It's what we create, partake, and explore in order to itch at the void
> to celebrate humanity
> It isn't a matter of whether it's good.
> It's a matter of what is it good for.*

"What is art?" How do you now answer the question, and how will your students?

---

*Line 1: Frank Neher (Yale Art Gallery, 2007), Line 2: Kate Williams (Yale Art Gallery 2007), Line 3: Andrew Houck (Yale Art Gallery, 2007), Lines 4–6: Adam Horowitz (Yale Art Gallery, 2007), Lines 7–8: Pete Seeger (*Democracy Now*, 2006)

REFERENCES

Alÿs, F. (2005). *Sometimes doing something poetic can become political and sometimes doing something political can become poetic.* New York: David Zwirner.

Art 21: Art in the 21st century (seasons 1 and 2). (2003). [Television series.] United States: PBS.

Bedford Gallery. (2009). *Bedford gallery: Past exhibitions.* Retrieved February 26, 2009, from http://www.bedfordgallery.org/past.htm

Democracy Now. (2006, September 4). *We shall overcome: An hour with legendary folk singer and activist Pete Seeger.* Retrieved October 23, 2007, from http://www.democracynow. org/2006/9/4/we_shall_overcome_an_hour_with.

Democracy Now. (2007, January 16). *Bill Moyers: "Big media is ravenous."* Retrieved January 4, 2008, from http://www.democracynow.org/2007/1/16/bill_moyers_big_ media_is_ravenous.

Epstein, R. (1999). Mindful practice. *Journal of the American Medical Association, 282,* 833–839.

Goldsworthy, A. (2001). *Midsummer snowballs.* New York: Harry N. Abrams.

Greenpeace. (2000). *Greenpeace backs "wonderful" giant snowball art.* Retrieved July 10, 2008, from http://www.greenpeace.org.uk/media/press-releases/greenpeace-backs-wonderful-giant-snowball-art

Hartigan, L. (2007). *Joseph Cornell: Navigating the imagination.* New Haven, CT: Yale University Press.

High and low, modern art and popular culture. (1990). New York: Museum of Modern Art exhibition guide.

Kahn, A. (2007). *Mick Jagger: A stone alone.* Retrieved January 4, 2008, from http://www. npr.org/templates/story/story.php?storyId=15524832

KQED Arts (2009). Gallery crawl. Bedford Gallery. Retrieved February 26, 2009, from http://www.kqed.org/arts/programs/gallerycrawl/profile.jsp?essid=22596

Lehrer, J. (2007, April 29). Hearts & minds. *The Boston Globe.* Retrieved January 4, 2008, from http://www.boston.com/news/education/higher/articles/2007/04/29/hearts__minds

Mackey, S. (2008, April 4). *Citywater.* Program notes for performance at University of California, Berkeley.

Payne, M. (2007). *Arctic winds.* Music premiered October 21, 2007, at Mills College, Oakland, CA.

Redding, L. (2007, October 19). *Post-performance discussion with Arnie Zane and Bill T. Jones and Company.* Presented at Yerba Buena Center for the Arts, San Francisco.

Souter, G. (2007). *Frida Kahlo and Diego Rivera.* New York: Parkstone Press.

Vygotsky, L. (1978). *Mind in society: The development of higher psychological processes.* Cambridge, MA: Harvard University Press.

Yale Art Gallery. (2007). *What is art and why does it matter?* Retrieved January 4, 2008, from http://artgallery.yale.edu/pages/whatisart/what_openhouse.html

CHAPTER 2

How Does Art Connect to Social Justice?

David M. Donahue, Jennifer Stuart, Todd Elkin, and Arzu Mistry

A T THE BEGINNING of the year, one of our teacher education students confided her disappointment about the emphasis on integrating the arts in the curriculum course we were teaching. She said, "I came to this teacher preparation program because I care about social justice. But when I heard you were going to be making the arts the center of this course, I felt cheated because the arts aren't really connected to social justice." If this student hadn't been such a smart and confident teacher, we might have dismissed her comments. Instead they've stayed with us. And a survey of our teacher education students at the end of the same year confirms that the arts are not high on the list of priorities in teaching for social justice. Integrating the arts ranked, on average, 6 out of 10 possible ways to teach for social justice behind other priorities like "creating a safe and inclusive classroom" and "teaching critical thinking."

When you think of art, does it bring to mind visions of stuffy museums and multimillion-dollar auctions at Christie's and Sotheby's? In a word, does art seem elitist? Or do you think of it as the strategy of least resistance for teachers who work with English language learners, fail to develop their academic language skills, and ask them to draw pictures instead? In other words, does art in school sometimes seem to be part of intentional or unintentional classism and racism? Or, especially for those of you teaching in urban schools, do you hear colleagues place the arts in false contrast to rigorous academic content that is seen as more likely to lead to college, well-paying jobs, and the kind of critical thinking valued by many teachers for social justice? Does art seem to be part of a conspiracy to withhold knowledge from poor students and students of color? This chapter will present an alternative picture of the arts, arts integration, and the connection between the arts and working for social justice.

In this chapter, we will reflect on the connections between arts integration and social justice in order to identify and dispel some of these misperceptions. The first section provides information on the role of art and artists in social change.

The purpose of this section is not to provide you with an overview of artists and activists or art that has sparked social change, but to challenge assumptions you may have about art as separate from social justice. The next section considers what it looks like from a social justice perspective to incorporate artwork and the processes of making art in the classroom. The final sections consider two promising strategies, community arts and service learning, as means for connecting arts education and arts integration with social justice.

ART AND SOCIAL JUSTICE

Think of what you need to live a life of dignity and record your list. What kinds of things did you think of? Some define human rights as what we need to live with dignity. Did you list education? The arts? Both are fundamental human rights and part of a life of dignity. Article 26 of the Universal Declaration of Human Rights says, "Everyone has the right to education" and "Education shall be directed to the full development of the human personality and to the strengthening of respect for human rights and fundamental freedoms. It shall promote understanding, tolerance and friendship among all nations, [and] racial or religious groups." Article 27 guarantees that "everyone has the right freely to participate in the cultural life of the community [and] to enjoy the arts."

Human rights are inalienable, indivisible, and interconnected (Flowers, 1998). Inalienable means education and the arts are rights not because a government chooses to give them to you but because you were born with a right to them. Indivisible means no one can say some rights are more important than others. This is particularly important for education and the arts. No government can say for any reason that other rights are more important than education or the arts. And rights are interconnected, meaning that without education you cannot fully enjoy the arts; without the arts, you are not fully educated. Because the arts are part of our human rights, they are also an integral part of education based on social justice.

The arts have long been connected to issues of justice. Whether artists consider themselves social or political activists, Burnham points out, "an artwork cannot be made that is separate from life." She continues, "Context, frame of reference, gender, cultural differences, and political realities have been revealed as part of every artwork" (quoted in Whittaker, 1993, sec. 2, para. 4). Speaking to this political dimension to art, historian and social justice advocate Howard Zinn describes the work of artists in times of inequality and injustice as transcendent. "The role of the artist is to transcend conventional wisdom, to transcend the word of the establishment, to transcend the orthodoxy, to go beyond and escape what is handed down by the government or what is said in the media" (Zinn, 2003, p. 11).

Artists have raised a number of issues and questions related to social justice. They have made visible and helped define people's identities, particularly those on the margins of power. They have named and documented injustice. They have provided alternative perspectives and raised prophetic voices to envision a better future. In the language of the studio habits of mind (Hetland, Winner, Veenema, & Sheridan, 2007), social justice artists and educators observe and express as well as reflect and envision. Spehler and Slattery (1999) describe the connection between these aspects of education and the arts:

> As educators concerned about making a difference in the world, we seek to create a different kind of space for the young to learn and grow. The arts are primary in this space because of their ability to develop voice, sustain passion, and evoke response. (p. 3)

The following examples illustrate how artists have engaged the public in social justice questions through their art. Mainly culled from the visual arts, they are meant to be illustrative, not to imply the sum total of art addressing questions of identity, injustice, or a better future. As you read about these examples, think about other works from a wide array of arts from music and drama to sculpture and performance that address similar issues. And next time you are in a museum, listening to music, or watching a play, think about art's connection to an aspect of social justice.

Identity

Questions of identity are central to the work of many artists. Questions of identity also matter to elementary and middle school children. They are discovering who they are, not only as individuals, but as members of communities defined by race, gender, and language. And in our current world, such aspects of identity carry different amounts of privilege. They also represent funds of knowledge (González & Moll, 2002; Moll, Amanti, Neff, & Gonzalez, 1992) from which teachers can draw.

An appreciation of identity inspires Chicana artist Margaret García. In a series of 16 paintings, *Un Nuevo Mestizaje* (1987–2001), García portrays Chicano men and women in all their diversity. Brought together, the paintings illustrate a community that cannot be defined in generalities. Speaking about the series, she says, "I have been documenting my community one at a time . . . to reveal the individual within the community. To see us one at a time, without clichés or stereotypes" (quoted in Romo, 2002, p. 27).

Similarly, photographer Glodean Champion's images inspired by a Nina Simone song, "Four Women," also address questions of identity, diversity, and commonality. Each of the four illustrations, Simone (shown), Aunt Sarah, Sweet Thing, and Peaches, depicts the same woman with different shades and hues because as Champion writes, "The only thing that separates us (Black Women) is our skin tone. We all view and are viewed by the society through the same lenses, some negative and some positive. It is our responsibility to hold on to the things that strengthen and uplift us and release those that attempt to weaken our resolve." (personal communication, December 4, 2009).

Figure 2.1. *Saffronia*, **from Four Women Collection, Glodean Champion, based on the song by Nina Simone.**

Naming Injustice

Artists have used their work to name and document social and political problems. Opening people's eyes, their work then became catalysts for addressing specific problems and making sure such injustices did not occur again. Similarly, young people in elementary and middle school are aware of social injustice issues in their classroom and the world. They recognize what is fair and are not afraid to call out what is not.

Goya is a perfect example of an artist who gave shape to his world through art naming injustice. Goya's paintings, drawings, and prints embody his critical thinking as well as his passionate feelings about his world. He was driven to make art not only by the economic imperatives of survival as an artist but also by deeply held moral beliefs. In the print series *Los Caprichos* and *Disasters of War*, Goya conveyed satirical ideas about the times in which he lived and visions representing the horror and violence that war visits upon humanity. These prints were not only formal exemplars of draftsmanship and the medium of etching, but also masterful works of narrative art filled with dark and resonant symbolism. Goya made *Los Caprichos* and *The Disasters of War* because his independent moral conscience drove him to speak out, through his artwork, about pivotal events shaping his time and place (Hughes, 2003). Goya's painting *The Third of May* is another work that conveys his passionate feelings about issues of war and justice.

This painting's iconic figure in white is one of the strongest and most galvanizing antiwar images in art. With this and other "Black Paintings" created near

Figure 2.2. *The Third of May,* **Goya, 1808.**

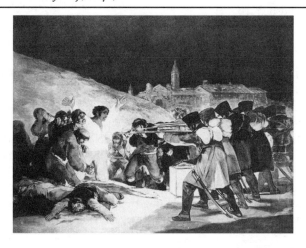

the end of his life, Goya tackled thoughts, questions, and feelings about mortality, spirituality, and the evil of war (Hughes, 2003).

More recently, during the La Raza movement of the 1960s and 1970s, Chicano mural artists named injustice and called for action. As Benevidez (2002) writes, "Paulo Freire, the Brazilian philosopher and proponent of education for critical consciousness, would have felt right at home on a street in East Los Angeles with

Figure 2.3. Fox Court, Eduardo Pineda and Joaquin Alejandro Newman, 2009.

Photo by Eduardo Pineda.

giant murals of farm workers and the words 'Boycott Gallo' in large letters floating above the bloodshed" (p. 17).

Continuing in that tradition of mural arts, "digital artists/digital discontents" John Leaños, Mónica Praba Pilar, and René Garcia collaborated on *Los Cybrids, La Raza Techno-Critica*, a series of temporary computer-generated murals about the intersection of technology, culture, and the "digital divide" (Creative Work Fund, 2001).

Another contemporary work, the Fox Courts murals painted in 2009, gave youth a voice in the burgeoning uptown neighborhood of Oakland, California. Muralists Eduardo Pineda and Joaquin Alejandro Newman worked with students at the Oakland School for the Arts in the community mural tradition of hands-on learning to express community ideals. Students modeled for the figures and created the imaginary fashions they wear. The mural, on an affordable living apartment building, is a reminder of how long-time residents of such newly popular neighborhoods can suffer from the injustice of gentrification.

Providing a Vision

Zinn (2003) describes how artists provide alternative visions of what a more just future might look like. By working "outside the framework that society has created, . . . the artist is taking us away from the moments of horror that we experience everyday—some days more than others—by showing us what is possible" (pp. 7–8). Like artists, young people in elementary and middle school can also think outside the usual frameworks. Not as bound as adults by the way things are, they can better envision and express the way they ought to be.

Diego Rivera's mural *Pan-American Unity* is an example of art by a painter and social activist whose work, not without controversy, portrayed injustice and presented images of a more hopeful future. Rivera illustrates the melding of craft and art from Latin America on the left side of the mural with the industry and technology of the United States on the right side. Uniting these two halves is a huge figure—part Aztec god, part industrial machine—representing the two parts of the hemisphere coming together. Speaking about what is possible as depicted in his mural, Rivera said, "I do not think that the capacity for artistic expression has anything to do with race or heredity. Opportunity, merely" (Rivera, quoted in Puccinelli, 1940, para. 5). Rivera's mural not only portrays unity between the two halves of the Western hemisphere, it argues that art can become a regular and meaningful part of our lives.

More recently, artists in the collaborative Futurefarmers work with a variety of media from installations to video games to pose questions and offer new perspectives on our relationship to the environment. They help viewers envision a more ecological future in pieces like *Bikebarrow*, part of a "utopian urban gardening proposal" and "Lunchbox Laboratory" (Futurefarmers, 2008), which provides young students with the opportunity to identify strains of algae that can be used

Figure 2.4. *Victory Gardens Bike Barrow*, **Futurefarmers, 2007.**

Photo by Amy Franceshini.

for renewable energy. In the dramatic arts, Freire served as inspiration for Augusto Boal (1985) and the "theater of the oppressed," which uses theater to help the oppressed move from spectators to "spect-actors" who become empowered to act against injustice and build a more peaceful, equitable, and just world.

INCORPORATING ARTWORKS IN THE SOCIAL JUSTICE CLASSROOM

Just as artists use their work to explore identity, name injustice, and offer a vision of justice, so, too, teachers committed to social justice can use arts-integrated curriculum toward such ends. One way to do so is to incorporate art like that mentioned in the previous section as a way to explore historical and contemporary social justice issues. For example, to explore identity in an integrated art and writing lesson, students might write about significant events in their own life and important elements of one of those events that shaped who they are. Simultaneously, they would also make a diorama about that important event in their life in the style of Pepón Osorio's *Tina's House*, which tells the story of a house fire's effect on one family. By comparing what they observe and express in both the art and the writing, students set the next stage in further developing one or both pieces of work. Born in Puerto Rico and drawing on his experience as a social worker in the Bronx, Osorio creates art in collaboration with the community, in keeping with his own principles of art and social justice. He says, "My principal commitment as an artist is to return art to the community" (*Art: 21*, 2001).

To name injustice, students might look at the work of William Kentridge, a South African artist, who explores issues of poverty and racism in his own country

(Rosenthal, 2009). Using techniques and materials similar to Kentridge's, students would then produce works on paper with charcoal and eraser to convey their perspective on issues in the community.

To provide a vision of the future, students might explore works such as Judy Chicago's *Envisioning the Future* project (Brown, 2004), which brings together visual art, multimedia, sculpture, and music from over 70 artists. In addition to the work itself, students might consider how the process of its creation, participatory art pedagogy, reflects a vision of cooperation and collaboration. Simultaneously, they could be reading literature ranging from poetry to science fiction that describes the future. As the culminating activity in the lesson, students could collaborate in a similar "envisioning the future" project depicting their own vision of a just and peaceful future.

What artwork moves you in its depiction of community, injustice, or future vision? How might you use it in your teaching to spark new ways of thinking or deeper understanding by your students?

INCORPORATING ART PROCESSES
IN THE SOCIAL JUSTICE CLASSROOM

While actual works of art can play a role in educating for social justice, the processes of art are also central to developing a social justice classroom. Heck (2001) describes how making art offers a metaphor for creating a classroom where multicultural identities and social justice are explored. Both require intrapersonal dialogue, problem-solving, risk-taking, interpersonal dialogue, equitable exchanges, evaluation and critical thinking, criticism/judgment, collaboration, creative thinking, and ongoing dialogue.

When opportunities are carefully crafted, making art can provide even the youngest students with multiple entry points into understanding complex social issues. Second graders at ASCEND School, an arts-integrated small school in Oakland, California, wrote a script, made shadow puppets, and created the music for *The Rise, Fall, and Ascent of Peralta Creek*, a culminating project that represented their research on the plant and animal ecology of their neighborhood creek. Peralta Creek runs three blocks from the ASCEND school, but prior to this study, the students in the second-grade class, many of whom live in the neighborhood, thought the creek was an open drain.

Second-grade teachers Hatti Saunders and Opus Wilson collaborated with music teacher Sarah Willner and visual art teacher Arzu Mistry to build students' understanding of the role of humans in sustaining or destroying the environments of a neighborhood. In classroom books and videos, students had seen many creek plants and animals before they saw the real creek. But the barren stream bore little similarity to the students' emerging understanding about creek ecology based on images and descriptions they had seen in the classroom. Where were the frogs, willow trees, and fish? Why was there so much trash? The juxtaposition of the ideal creek the students had expected, in contrast to the reality they had witnessed, provoked students to explore their questions—the basis of social critique.

The students set to work writing questions and thoughts about the creek, researching the creek from both a scientific and historical perspective, creating puppets to bring their newly developed story of the creek to life, composing music and sounds that represented the story of the creek, and putting on a play for the school community. Students really understood the impact of their sustained efforts when they were asked to present *The Rise, Fall, and Ascent of Peralta Creek* at a board meeting of the Urban Creek Council. They were stunned and thrilled by the opportunity to share their views and understanding with the adult community. In this way, the art making and the learning environment of the classroom mirror the qualities described by Heck (2001) as central to social justice.

Think of times you have incorporated making art into a lesson or seen another teacher do so. Can you find the elements of Heck's multicultural, social justice classroom in the activity? If so, what are they? How did the process of making art contribute to them? If not, where were the lost opportunities? How might the lesson be taught differently to accentuate the qualities of a social justice classroom?

Artworks about social justice and art processes are two ways to think about the intersection of the arts and social justice but they are not mutually exclusive. Both can be and often are part of social justice art. In other words, art about social justice can grow out of collective visions of justice and creative collaboration, not just an individual artist's vision and work. Similarly, when artists seek to communicate understanding about social justice through art, they may find that the process of creating their art becomes as important as the final product in fostering peace, nurturing equity, or giving voice to the marginalized. The next sections of this chapter describe two movements in art and social justice—community arts and arts-based service learning—that illustrate the connections between art processes and products and the possibilities for making these connections in the curriculum.

COMMUNITY ARTS

Community arts has been described as "art in other places" (Cleveland, 2000), meaning art that has moved out of the museum and into the communities, agencies, and institutions where it can have a direct, positive impact on the lives of people, from the most personal to the most political levels. As described by Mesa-Bains, community art not only seeks to improve people's individual and collective lives, it grows out of those lives:

> Art is a transformative practice that arises from people's struggles to make sense of the world. Art is a language and a form in which people express their deepest needs

and beliefs, and in doing so, art lives for them. It is not something put in a building for which you pay to get a glimpse, but do not even receive an explanation. It is the set of practices concerning people's life choices. (Bains & Mesa-Bains, 2002, p. 184)

Community artists believe that the process of their art is as important as the resulting artwork in promoting social justice. Speaking to artists and the communities they work with, deNobriga and Schwarzman (1999) write, "If we want freedom, we must promote free expression. If we want equity, we must have equal access and support in expressing ourselves. If we want respect and love and beauty among us and all our many communities, we must actively and systematically promote it through our art and through our teaching of others" (para. 4). In an era when so much work to eradicate poverty and develop communities is based on the needs or perceived "deficits" of people marginalized by those with power (Kretzmann & McKnight, 1993), community artists work from the assets and strengths of a community.

You can incorporate community arts in your classroom by working with a teaching artist who practices community arts. Your students will then become the voice of their community as they and the teaching artist collaborate. If you cannot work with a teaching artist, you can draw on the spirit of community arts by creating projects that address community concerns, encourage community participation and feedback, or honor an intentional collaborative process of working as a class to make one piece of art.

SERVICE LEARNING

Service learning, an educational strategy to meet genuine human needs in combination with explicit attention to learning from service, is another way to bring together art and social justice. Several social justice themes stand out in service learning: collaborating with the community, developing civic and social responsibility, crossing various boundaries of identity such as race and disability, learning empathy for others, honoring multiple perspectives, and creating reciprocal relationships. Given these themes, service learning shares many qualities with community arts and some community arts projects can be service learning projects, and vice versa. The time frame of service learning projects can range from one afternoon where university students accompany young people on a walking tour of neighborhood murals to a yearlong project of planning and making a mural. The longer the duration of the project, the greater the possibilities for developing meaningful, reciprocal relations and deeper reflection on learning from service.

As you think about community arts and art-based service learning, compare them to your own experiences, either as a student or a teacher, with art in the classroom. What stands out as similar? What stands out as different? For many, the collaborative nature of community arts and service learning probably departs from our own experiences of making art in school, where the emphasis was placed on creating individual products. For others, the attention to process as equally important to product may stand in contrast to art making in school, where the goal was to create a piece that looked a certain way and where less attention was paid to thinking about the relationship with others or dialogue sparked by the piece's creation. What do you see as the implications of community arts and service learning for your own teaching for social justice? Perhaps you realize that teaching for social justice, whether arts based or not, is stronger in collaboration with others from the community. Maybe you see the importance of multiple perspectives to gain meaning from or give meaning to art and to questions of social justice. Or you may see that the social justice aspect of art has as much to do with reflecting on every step of its creation as it does with the final work. If making, viewing, or even thinking about art has made you think of new questions, dilemmas, or angles on social justice issues, then you can begin to appreciate the power of art to promote the habits of mind necessary for a more just and equitable world.

REFERENCES

Art: 21. (2001). *Pepón Osorio biography.* Retrieved August 9, 2008, from http://www.pbs.org/art21/artists/osorio/index.html

Bains, R., & Mesa-Bains, A. (2002). A reciprocal university: A model for arts, justice, and community. *Social Justice, 29*(4), 182–197.

Benavidez, M. (2002). Chicano art: Culture, myth, and sensibility. In C. Marin (Ed.), *Chicano visions: American painters on the verge* (pp. 11–12). Boston: Little, Brown.

Boal, A. (1985). *Theatre of the oppressed.* New York: Theatre Communications Group.

Brown, B. (2004). *Judy Chicago's "Envisioning the Future."* Retrieved August 10, 2008, from http://artscenecal.com/ArticlesFile/Archive/Articles2004/Articles0204/JChicagoB.html

Cleveland, W. (2000). *Art in other places: Artists at work in America's community and social institutions.* New York: Praeger.

Creative Work Fund. (2001). *Los Cybrids, La Raza techno-critica.* Retrieved August 9, 2008, from http://www.creativeworkfund.org/pages/bios/john_leanos.html

deNobriga, K., & Schwarzman, M. (1999). Community-based art for social change. In *The community arts training directory.* Retrieved July 21, 2006, from http://www.communityarts.net/archivefiles/education/index/php

Flowers, N. (1998). *Human rights here and now: Celebrating the Universal Declaration of Human Rights.* New York: Human Rights Educator's Network, Amnesty International USA.

Futurefarmers. (2008). Futurefarmers project site. Retrieved August 9, 2008, from http://www.futurefarmers.com/survey/

González, N., & Moll, L. (2002). Cruzando el puente: Building Bridges to funds of knowledge. *Educational Policy, 16*(4), 623–641.

Heck, M. L. (2001). Eye messages: A partnership of artmaking and multicultural education. *Multicultural Perspectives, 3*(1), 3–8.

Hetland, L., Winner, E., Veenema, S., & Sheridan, K. (2007). *Studio thinking: The real benefits of visual arts education.* New York: Teachers College Press.

Hughes, R. (2003). *Goya.* New York: Alfred A. Knopf.

Kretzmann, J., & McKnight, J. (1993). *Building communities from the inside out: A path toward funding and mobilizing a community's assets.* Chicago: Acta.

Moll, L., Amanti, C., Neff, D., & Gonzalez, N. (1992). Funds of knowledge for teaching: Using a qualitative approach to connect homes and classrooms. *Theory into Practice, 31*(2), 132–141.

Puccinelli, D. (1940). *Diego Rivera on Pan American Unity* . . . Interview with Diego Rivera, San Francisco, CA. Retrieved July 26, 2006, from http://www.riveramural.org/article.asp?section=mural&key=1000&language=english

Romo, T. (2002). Mestiza aesthetics and Chicana painterly visions. In C. Marin (Ed.), *Chicano visions: American painters on the verge* (pp. 23–31) Boston: Little, Brown.

Rosenthal, M. (Ed.). (2009). *William Kentridge: Five themes.* New Haven, CT: Yale University Press.

Spehler, R. M., & Slattery, P. (1999). Voices of imagination: The artist as prophet in the process of social change. *International Journal of Leadership in Education, 2*(1), 1–12.

Whittaker, B. (1993). The arts of social change: Artistic, philosophical, and managerial issues. *Journal of Arts Management, Law, & Society, 23*(1), 25–35. Retrieved May 30, 2006, from http://search.epnet.com/login.aspx?direct=true&db=aph&an9706250250

Zinn, H. (2003). *Artists in times of war.* New York: Seven Stories Press.

PART II

Art for Every Child

CHAPTER 3

Creating Alliances for Arts Learning and Arts Integration

Louise Music

I LEARNED ABOUT arts learning and community as a classroom teacher who taught art every day and integrated the arts into student learning for 5-, 6-, and 7-year-olds. I believed, based on my experience as a teacher, mother, and artist, that the arts were essential to children making meaning of their experience and the world around them.

In my classroom, students studied the mobiles and stabiles of Alexander Calder and learned about balance, symmetry, and the foundational concepts of physics. They studied the paintings of Jacob Lawrence and learned about the African diaspora, connecting it to the movement and immigration of their own parents, grandparents, and great-grandparents. They met authors like Patricia Palacco, and by mid–first grade had all written their own hardbound books that sat on the bookshelf for their classmates to choose during reading time. They studied the frogs that lived in a tank in our classroom and garden snails that left a trail on their desks. They made observational and anatomical drawings, while learning about the habitats and ecology of these animals' environments.

All the 5-, 6-, and 7-year-olds in my classroom drew, painted, created, performed, sang, and danced as a regular means of developing and communicating their evolving skills, knowledge, and identities as mathematicians, historians, scientists, authors, and community members.

Classrooms like this require planning and collaboration. I was lucky to have a veteran primary school teacher as my team teacher. Together we developed long-term integrated units; involved families and parents as co-teachers and co-planners; created community-wide events and projects; took field trips to museums, libraries, and local watersheds; and engaged our kindergartners and first graders as thinkers, planners, artists, and problem solvers. Working in a city school, we recognized the futility in bemoaning a lack of resources or support. We looked around our classrooms and community and tapped the rich human resources of our students, their families, and our neighborhood. We discovered that we had everything we needed right within our community and could draw on the eagerness of our students to learn, the cultural gifts of our students' families, and the arts-learning resources of our museums and artist communities. We had so many more resources than we could possibly utilize fully, and well, at any one time. These same conditions exist for all of us, no matter our classroom or learning community, if we only look.

About the time that I left my job teaching this multiage kindergarten–first-grade class to work at the Alameda County Office of Education, I read a book called *A Simple Justice* (Ayers, Klonsky, & Lyon, 2000). The book includes stories of activists and teacher leaders imagining a new place for the intersection of teaching, learning, equity, and the dream for creating a future in which we can all live productively and joyfully. In the introduction, Ayers suggests:

> A primary challenge to teachers is to see students as three dimensional creatures . . . with hopes, dreams, aspirations, skills and capacities; with bodies, minds, hearts and spirits; with experiences, histories, a past, a pathway and a future; with a family, a community, a language and a culture. This knotty, complicated challenge requires patience, curiosity, wonder, awe and humility. It demands sustained focus, intelligent judgment, inquiry and investigation. (p. 2)

He concludes, "We must embrace and organize every potential ally" (p. 6).

Reading this, I was inspired. I see the languages of the arts as a means for every child to be seen fully, more than a numerical statistic or a flat category of "proficient" or "far below basic." I believe that rather than a single view of what it means for students to come to school "prepared," we as educators need to build the cultural competency to work with parents to understand who every child is. We need to recognize the rich set of experiences and the history that all children bring to school from their lived experience. Teachers need strategies and skills to create multiple entry points into classroom curriculum, building on the cultural gifts children bring from their families and communities.

I also know that simply engaging students in wonderful arts learning experiences is not enough. We need to work with arts educators to aim the rich and engaging experiences of the arts at important educational goals set by teachers, administrators, and school communities, so that students can gain the educational advantage necessary to build strong neighborhoods and communities. I wanted to be part of a big change to create the world Ayers described, and I wondered what part I could play. The role I have chosen is to bring people together, to build alliances for arts learning.

The arts learning and integration described throughout this book does not occur in a vacuum. While many teachers view their classrooms as their own domain once the door is closed, we can only accomplish so much on our own. Making schools equitable and joyful places of rigorous, meaningful learning for all students is an enormous task, and we cannot do it alone.

In this chapter, I share details of how allies came together in Alameda County, where I am the visual and performing arts education coordinator at the Alameda County Office of Education, to illustrate that coalition building is not only necessary, but also possible. I use the examples of coalition building as texts for questioning and reflecting so you can also think about how to create an environment for arts learning and build coalitions that can accomplish more in your community than any of us can by working alone.

CREATING AN ENVIRONMENT FOR ARTS LEARNING AND COALITION BUILDING

The door to coalition building for arts education and integration in Alameda County was opened in 1998 by Sheila Jordan, the new superintendent of schools. As a previous school board and city council member, she had worked with artists to create community and purpose for young people through performance art events such as Code 33, which assembled 200 youth on the roof of a downtown Oakland parking garage to talk with Oakland police officers about stopping violence and creating trusting relationships between police and young people in their neighborhoods (Roth, 2001). She became convinced that every child had the right to an education that included the arts, and she created a position for a visual and performing arts coordinator at the Alameda County Office of Education to give arts education greater visibility and legitimacy.

This "door opening" reveals two important lessons. First, you can begin to make climate change even with only one other ally as you build your coalition. Second, give potential allies powerful examples of arts learning like the Code 33 event to ensure success. Start to consider who might be your first ally. What are the events or projects already taking place or in the planning stages in your school or community that might yield a champion and begin to galvanize a coalition?

Also in 1998, the California School Board adopted state standards for visual and performing arts, and California universities and state universities began requiring 1 year of visual and performing arts at the high school level for entrance. These new policies built momentum for arts in schools. If California schools were going to support students to meet college entrance requirements, addressing the lack of arts education and teacher capacity to teach the arts in K–12 schools had to be addressed. This gave our efforts added legitimacy.

As you begin building a coalition, consider the policy environment and how it can be used to your advantage. Use high school exit and college entrance requirements in the arts as a lever for bringing partners on board for arts learning.

BEGIN WHERE YOU ARE WITH WHAT YOU HAVE

Just as children benefit from differentiated instruction, every school and every district has different needs, different resources, different challenges, and different starting places. Many of our students speak a language other than English as their first language; perhaps your district is composed of small schools in isolated rural locations; perhaps you live in an area rich in artists and cultural resources; or perhaps the nearest bookstore is several hours away.

Alameda County is located just east of San Francisco and encompasses 18 public school districts. The districts range from Oakland, a large inner-city district, to Mountain House, a rural one-school district. Where there was a district-level administrator with responsibilities for the visual and performing arts, we worked with that person. In other districts, we started with an enthusiastic principal, teacher, or parent to build a district arts team. Each of these districts started somewhere and built upon what it had.

District or school communities need to establish a common vision for the role of arts education in supporting student learning and development that involves all stakeholders in order to ensure that all students have opportunities to experience quality learning in every school, every day. The vision will reinforce the values and priorities of the community and serve as a mechanism to build consensus, enthusiasm, and endorsement among stakeholders. Stakeholders may include teachers (classroom and arts specialists), administrators (site based and district level), superintendent/assistant superintendent(s), parents, students, community business leaders, artists and representatives of arts organizations, school board members, and representatives from higher education.

The vision reflects the values of educators, parents, students, and the business community, and that combined vision enables the creation of a plan. The plan should include agreement on the skills, knowledge, and dispositions that every student needs in order to be successful in school today.

We used a simple plan to create a vision: We asked people what matters most to them in their school, district, or county and collected their ideas in short phrases. We grouped common ideas together and agreed on the theme of each group. A smaller committee then crafted the vision for group review based on the themes.

BRING THE PRIMARY PARTNERS TOGETHER

As the first full-time visual and performing arts coordinator in Alameda County, I began to identify others—teachers, artists, superintendents, and parents—who were making efforts to provide more access for arts in schools, even as some claimed that this could not be a priority in the current educational environment. I met with arts educators, ranging from high school art teachers to educators in museums and community arts organizations, who were keeping the light of imaginative and creative thought alive in our schools through residencies and after-school programs. We discussed how the county education office could help in their efforts and how, together, we could make the case for arts learning and arts integration as a means to assure that no child is denied the opportunity of a high-quality education and the opportunity for access to higher education.

A group of arts education organizations, including the Alameda County Arts Commission, the Oakland Museum, the Museum of Children's Art, Luna Kids Dance, Opera Piccola, the California College of the Arts, the Berkeley Repertory Theatre, the Oakland Youth Chorus, Destiny Arts, Art Esteem, the East Bay Children's Theatre, His Majesties' Musicians, the California Arts Project, and others, began meeting monthly to network with schools and districts and to plan for an annual monthlong showcase of youth learning in the arts. We called our showcase Art *IS* Education! envisioning a series of exhibitions and performances of learning in and through the arts at school and community venues. We wanted a forum for arts educators to partner with classroom teachers and students to highlight how students are learning in the arts and advance the message that art is, indeed, education. We planned for audiences of parents, community members, and policymakers to interact with public presentations of students' arts learning so that they could see how learning in and through the arts accomplishes larger educational goals. Our strategy is based on a social change theory that a unified message, based on shared public values, connected to examples of good practice, will create a "tipping point" (Gladwell, 2002).

The meetings also led to forming the Alameda County Alliance for Arts Learning Leadership (Alliance for ALL). As the teachers, arists, principals, parents, community members, funders, policymakers, and teacher educators participate in the work of the alliance, they become leaders in their own communities and advocates for a fair and simple goal—that all children, not just the lucky or the privileged, have access to a meaningful education with arts learning at the center. The Alliance for ALL became a center of information and inspiration for teachers, schools, and districts.

BUILD RELATIONSHIPS WITH DIVERSE PARTNERS

We used our shared beliefs and eagerness to work together to reach out to teachers and teaching artists, principals, parents, and institutions of higher education.

Teachers and Teaching Artists as Partners

Teachers and teaching artists are our central partners; they make the choices and decisions from moment to moment that can capture students' attention and engage them thoughtfully in important experiences. When they work together in the alliance, teachers and artists co-mentor each other in ways that advance artistry and teaching and that serve students directly.

As the work continues, new teacher-artist teams are included and prepare to share their work with a new generation of educators looking to take control of their practice. We seek to build the knowledge, skills, will, and capacity of arts organizations in this way to align arts-learning programs and experiences with the goals of educators in schools and districts and to situate arts learning squarely at the center of school reform and the transformation of education. Specifically, we bring school and arts leaders together to ask questions such as these:

- What shall we teach, and why does it matter?
- What do we want students to understand?
- What will we ask students to do to develop and deepen their understanding?
- How will we assess students' understanding in an ongoing way so that we can inform next steps in teaching?

Principals as Partners

Principals play an instrumental role in setting the course for how a vision for arts learning plays out for every child in action and policy. We work with like-minded principals who have a strong commitment to meeting students at their individual edges of academic, emotional, and social learning and who believe that every student can be successful in school today. These principals take risks, departing from a scripted curriculum that dictates what teachers should teach, to embrace a curriculum that honors and privileges the professional, inquiry-based nature of teaching and that engages the imagination of teachers and students.

In the alliance, we create times for principals to share their successes and challenges with their peers, both to inspire one another and to provide support for problem-solving and negotiating difficulties. We also support principals in clarifying and articulating what their school is trying to achieve for students generally, so that arts learning can be explicitly directed at desired student outcomes.

We see principals within the alliance who are successful in supporting arts education programs collaborating to do the following:

- Create a school environment that fosters equity and honors diverse cultural arts backgrounds and experiences.
- Provide opportunities for teachers to make arts learning visible and share student achievements.
- Establish partnerships with community arts organizations and arts practitioners.
- Allocate resources and ensure opportunities for teachers to engage in professional development, including time for planning and collaboration between teachers, arts specialists, and teaching artists.

Parents as Partners

We involve parents because they know who students are as individual human beings. They are essential partners if teachers are to build the cultural competency to understand what matters to students and how to create relevant classroom experiences.

In the alliance, we work directly with parents and parent groups through the Arts Active Parent Project. Arts Active Parents not only engage their own children in art, they believe that all kids learn better if they're creating and appreciating art, so they are advocates for every child to have access to arts programs in their schools and districts. We provide speakers' trainings so that parents can educate local policymakers by telling their own stories and bringing policymakers on site visits to observe successes and challenges in their schools' arts programs. To support parents in having a voice in the state budget allocation process, we convened an informational and strategic panel of parent activists and local legislators or their staff. Using the resources of the alliance Web site, we facilitated letter-writing campaigns to local and state legislators in support of quality arts education. We unite Arts Active Parents across school and district lines to create a regional voice that can help change schools for every child.

Higher Education Institutions as Partners

Partnerships with other educators, including university researchers and professional developers, are valuable because they allow us to learn and do the work better. Because arts education and integration are at the margins of schools, we too often focus partnerships on their own survival. In more supportive times, it can be just as easy to focus on expanding programs without really attending to making them better. Partnerships, like the ones we created with colleges and universities, help us think about quality. As you identify your partners and allies, remember to include those who will help you learn and improve.

For example, to do our work better, the Alliance for ALL partnered, through a grant from the U.S. Department of Education, with the California College of the Arts' Center for Art and Public Life and the Harvard Graduate School of Education's Project Zero in the Arts Learning Anchor School Initiative. Our goal was to convey what art teachers are teaching and what students are learning. The California College of the Arts offered alliance teachers resources, insight, and professional development about specific art practices, about partnerships with families, and about the role of contemporary art in art education.

Researchers from Project Zero at the Harvard Graduate School of Education contributed a different kind of expertise. They helped the community of school practitioners and arts providers build our local capacity by helping us learn to use research-based "thinking frames" (Perkins, 1986) such as Studio Thinking (Hetland, Winner, Veenema, & Sheridan, 2007) and Teaching for Understanding (Blythe & Researchers & Teachers, 1998; Wiske, 1998). These frames help us to understand and explain why we teach the arts, how the arts develop student thinking across all content areas, and how to better aim teaching in the arts intentionally toward understanding in the arts and across the curriculum.

The central frame for this work has been the Studio Thinking Framework, developed by Hetland, Winner, Veenema, and Sheridan (2007). The Studio

Thinking Framework identifies eight studio habits of mind (see Introduction) that illustrate explicitly what is being taught in arts classrooms beyond the development of skill and technique. We work with arts teachers to name, convey, and assess these habits that are uniquely cultivated in the arts and that are necessary for learning in all content areas and in life (Winner & Hetland, 2008).

We piloted Studio Thinking in Alameda County with arts teachers in five public schools in Oakland, Berkeley, and Emeryville. Together teachers and artists examined their own practice and collected data about it. Engaged teachers and artists met regularly with researchers from universities to look at data and ask, "What are we learning here?" Studio Thinking helped arts teachers and teaching artists learn to communicate the real benefit of arts education.

University researchers, teachers, and teaching artists generated new questions, interrogated issues of quality and equity, and identified next steps in practice. Teachers and artists became co-investigators with university researchers. Rather than research on teacher practice, this was research *with* teachers as equal partners.

Through our work with university partners, teachers and teaching artists continue to gain skills and build the confidence necessary to take on leadership roles at school sites, in arts organizations, and in public discourse. Our university partners help us continue to develop our capacity to use contemporary art purposefully and to assess learning in the arts not only in skill and technique, but also in various forms of thinking.

We used another Project Zero framework, Teaching for Understanding (Blythe et al., 1998; Wiske, 1998) to structure the online tool that teachers and teaching artists use to share their work with one another. Based on Teaching for Understanding, the online template helped teachers think clearly about student learning and convey learning in ways readily understood by a broad range of audiences. The common template gave us language to both think about and share a diversity of artistic approaches that teachers and teaching artists use as they work to integrate arts.

As you plan your own alliances, think about adapting or developing common frameworks and templates such as these for reflecting on and talking about arts learning, and then use those frameworks to think and talk about questions of arts learning that are important to all partners.

BROADEN YOUR THINKING ABOUT ALLIES

Look beyond your local community for allies. We have had successful partnerships with foundations, government agencies, nonprofit school reform organizations, and the business community.

Funders who can support your work are an important part of any alliance for arts education and integration. Alliance for ALL has worked with local and national foundations. Public funding opportunities from the U.S. and California Departments of Education, along with both local and national private foundations, have played a critical role in the development and sustainability of our work. We invite local funders to participate in our strategic planning processes. We use the resources of a national private foundation to connect to other national resources. The Alameda County Alliance for Arts Learning Leadership allows funders to connect their interests across communities through the partnerships that the alliance makes. Our approach meets the goals of many private foundations seeking to overcome isolated "silo approaches" within communities and within the foundations themselves. Arts learning in schools is a goal that has brought education and arts program officers together to better leverage foundation resources for embedded and lasting change in communities.

We also partner with the school reform and local small-schools movement. We saw alignment of our mission with the Bay Area Coalition for Equitable Schools to provide equitable access to a high-quality education, so we worked in new small schools to demonstrate the role of the arts in student, teacher, and community learning. For us, the small-schools advocates are natural allies because of a shared concern with reform, educational equity, and high standards for learning across all disciplines, not only the arts. We identify artists to plan arts-integrated curriculum that leverages learning with classroom teachers and connects quality arts and arts integration with English language acquisition and learning in other academic areas.

In addition, we partner with members of the business community. We no longer live in a world ruled by a finite canon of knowledge that will prepare young people for citizenship, careers, and lifelong satisfaction. Insights and projections into the 21st-century workforce tell us that the job market will increasingly require workers who are problem-solvers and innovators; they must be intellectually flexible, creative, and collaboratively inclined. All these dispositions and skills are intentionally and methodically cultivated in arts and cross-curricular arts-integrated learning environments.

Increasingly, the business community is coming to understand this changing job market, and now is the time to encourage the participation, advocacy, and support of the business sector in supporting arts education and improving public education. Business leaders can be invited to serve on district planning committees and arts teams. They can be recruited to create internships and job shadow programs that extend the classroom to the workplace. They can be cultivated to inform chambers of commerce, rotaries, and professional organizations on the impact of local arts education programs and garner organizational support to honor arts students and teachers and provide financial awards. They can lead efforts for local property taxes to support arts education and write editorial pieces in public newspapers about arts in schools and links to a healthy economy. They can be a persuasive voice and join with the broader community to call for public policies that fully fund public education, including the arts.

As you imagine your allies, think about the organizations and institutions in your community that share similar goals. And as you craft your own mission and goals, do so in ways that make explicit what you share in common with others. This makes building coalitions part of your work rather than a separate enterprise.

SHARE YOUR WORK WITH PARTNERS ACROSS THE FIELD

The alliance provides opportunities for teachers to share their work with colleagues and the public. For example, when teams of arts and nonarts teachers collaboratively plan for arts integration units, the Alliance for ALL helps these teacher teams make student learning visible (see Chapter 4, on making learning visible) through site-based and online documentation of the classroom arts-integration process. The teachers then share this learning with other educators and parents in a wide range of forums. In this way, the possibilities for arts learning to differentiate instruction and provide multiple means for students and teachers to have access to subject matter is demonstrated to principals, other teachers, and parents. This strategy helps us gain new allies for our efforts. Making student and classroom learning visible is *both* an embedded assessment strategy and an embedded advocacy strategy. The alliance actively pursues opportunities for teachers and teaching artists to highlight and share their work, for example, at regional and state gatherings and conferences, in formal presentations to school colleagues and parents, and through our online action research tool. By going public with our work, we hold ourselves accountable to our learning goals for every child and gain insights for next steps in instruction.

ADVOCATE FOR ARTS EDUCATION TO GAIN SUPPORT

A plethora of research suggests that students who learn in the arts are more likely to succeed in school (Burnaford, 2007; Deasy, 2002; Hetland et al., 2007). Yet the research did not convince broad groups of educators to change their practice, nor did it give them any tools about *how* they might change their practice if they were so inclined. To be effective, it is not enough to find allies who agree that the arts are an essential part of learning. It is necessary to find a means to communicate about why and how student learning in the arts helps achieve equitable access to a high-quality education.

The Alameda County Office of Education's Alliance for ALL has a countywide shared message that art *is* education! In this time of high-stakes testing, which places demands on educators' and policymakers' energy and attention to be accountable for learning outcomes for every child, the Alliance for ALL has had to make a case to every stakeholder that arts matter in schools, and then prove why they matter so much. Our ability to advocate not just for arts in schools, but also explicitly for student creative expression, engagement, and risk-taking, has been important for involving stakeholders in our public schools, who recognize how essential such skills and qualities are in our communities and our economy.

REMEMBER, ART *IS* PART OF A HIGH-QUALITY EDUCATION

As we hand over this world of complex and challenging problems to our children, we must provide them the tools to develop the creativity and flexibility to devise strategies we cannot imagine. Students need to do more than memorize information for recall. They must have the ability and inclination to apply new skills and knowledge and be alert to opportunities to apply what they know in novel situations as they advance through grade levels. The arts are human languages, essential for envisioning solutions and perceiving and communicating meaning, beauty, fear, and desire, as well as tools for planning and decision-making in a nuanced, ever-changing world. We owe it to our children, and to our collective future, to extend the creative opportunities to develop students' minds, to teach them to think, to imagine, and to discover solutions through the arts.

Through the alliance we have found effective ways to make arts education part of the strategy and narrative around accountability for a high-quality education for every child. We have helped teachers, community members, and policymakers to understand that there is no tension between providing access to a high-quality education for every child and access to arts education for every child; they are one and the same conversation. When arts in schools and accountability for student outcomes are presented as two side-by-side conversations that compete for resources and time in our public schools, we miss the real opportunity to argue for why the arts are essential to learning, why they matter in public schools, and why they matter as we prepare students in schools today for full participation in community and life tomorrow. By approaching the issues through a single conversation, arts educators in and out of schools partner with public school educators, parents, and policymakers for classroom practice that aligns with shared goals. Arts-learning educators and advocates articulate the value of learning in the arts, recognize that the arts can build on the history and experiences every child brings to school, and use arts to expand students' horizons and deepen learning across the content areas.

To build alliances with educators in other subject areas, we stress that quality arts-integrated environments embrace the learning styles and experience of every child and create multiple entry points for diverse communities of students to investigate English language arts, mathematics, science, and social studies through music, dance, drama, and visual arts. The arts are basic human languages, necessary to community development. They have persisted through humanity in times of prosperity and of despair and hardship (Dissanayake, 1990). Learning in and through the arts can help to ensure that every child is engaged in school and has the opportunity to advance according to his or her learning style.

The data emerging from the work of the alliance show us that teachers and administrators are united in their enthusiasm for tools that help them teach better, stay attuned to individual students' learning styles, and adjust their instructional practices. At the same time, students are being educated, through the practice and experience of the arts, in habits of mind essential to helping them gain entry to all academic subjects, for the educational advancement they absolutely must have to claim a life of civic engagement, social connectedness, and creativity.

If we are to achieve a shared vision of a high-quality education for every child, it will take a multitude of players with a singleness of purpose over a sustained period of time. That is why developing leadership at all levels—the leadership of parents, principals, classroom teachers, reform organizations, foundations, and policy makers—is vital to creating a shared vision for a positive future.

REFERENCES

Ayers, W., Klonsky, M., & Lyon, G. (2000). *A simple justice: The challenge of small schools.* New York: Teachers College Press.

Blythe, T., & the Researchers and Teachers of the Teaching for Understanding Project. (1998). *The teaching for understanding guide.* San Francisco: Jossey-Bass.

Burnaford, G. (2007). *Arts integration frameworks, research, and practice: A literature review.* Washington, DC: Arts Education Partnership

Deasy, R. (Ed.). (2002). *Critical links: Learning in the arts and student academic and social development.* Washington, DC: Arts Education Partnership.

Dissanayake, E. (1990). *What is art for?* Seattle: University of Washington Press

Gladwell, M. (2002). *The tipping point: How little things can make a big difference.* Boston: Back Bay Books.

Hetland, L., Winner, E., Veenema, S., & Sheridan, K. (2007). *Studio thinking: The real benefits of visual arts education.* New York: Teachers College.

Perkins, D. N. (1986). Thinking frames. *Educational Leadership, 43*(8), 4–10.

Roth, M. (2001). Making and performing Code 33: A public art project with Suzanne Lacy, Julio Morales, and Unique Holland. *PAJ, 69,* 67–83.

Winner, E., & Hetland, L. (2008). Art for our sake: School arts classes matter more than ever—but not for the reasons you think. *Arts Education Policy Review, 109*(5), 29–32.

Wiske, M. S. (Ed.). (1998). *Teaching for understanding: Linking research with practice.* San Francisco: Jossey-Bass.

CHAPTER 4

Seeing Is Believing

Making Our Learning Through the Arts Visible

Stephanie Violet Juno

L EARNING, LIKE falling in love or other significant changes that take place in that complex and not fully understood nexus of the mind/heart/body, is for the most part invisible. Like other teachers, teaching artists, and arts teachers, I have struggled with this challenge for years. As an educator, I am focused on my students' learning, but the transformational process itself is elusive. I know my students don't understand a concept when they wear a look of confusion or frustration. I know my students understand an idea when their faces glow and they can't wait to share it. However, those pivotal moments of learning that happen in between understanding and not understanding are often simply not apparent. This chapter describes how this invisible learning manifests in classrooms and shares examples of how you can start making your student learning visible.

In my experience, the challenge of invisible learning most often manifests itself in three ways. The first is the Parent Night Conundrum. This is that special time of the year designated to show parents what students have learned, but—here's the catch—without actually showing the learning process! Because parent night occurs after school hours when no normal school learning activity takes place, the focus is often on showing what students "have learned" rather than what they "are learning." Consequently, these events often feature plays or concerts, art exhibits, and bulletin boards of final essays and completed worksheets. Student accomplishment needs to be honored; however, a focus on learning is lost in the face of so much "product." It also sets the stage for the second manifestation, which I call the Wow Effect.

A common response from a parent about a finished artwork is simply "Wow!" Parents often view the presentation of student work as if it magically appeared full grown like Athena born from the head of Zeus. They exclaim, "Our kids are so talented!" or "I don't know how you got my kid to do that!" The answer to the implied question is that the children used their brilliant brains and a lot of practice. The awe-inspiring growth a child makes learning through the arts is often rendered invisible by the sheer glamour of the finished artwork, play, or concert. As educators, we face an inherent challenge when displaying finished artwork and hoping the entire learning process—which may have involved basic skill development, the challenges of group work, troubleshooting, and revision—might shine through to people who were never in the classroom witnessing it unfold.

However, perhaps most important to an educator is the third issue, that students do not generally, naturally, or effortlessly articulate their learning. They might be able to tell you and their parents if they "liked" acting in a play or "didn't like" an art project. When asked further about this, they might say it was "fun" or it was "too hard." When asked more specifically what they learned, they might point to quantifiable things like a particular song they learned to play on the violin or a piece of choreography they know how to dance or they might simply say, "Lots of stuff."

In the examples above, students are talking about their learning, albeit with a limited vocabulary, which leaves a lot open to interpretation. It is possible that when they say it was "fun," they mean that they enjoyed the process of being challenged by new ideas and that their eventual mastery of the new concepts gave them a sense of joy. Or when they say it was "too hard," they might mean that they found it difficult to stay engaged when they became frustrated with repeated attempts to master a new skill with only minimal improvement in their eyes. When they say they did "lots of stuff," they might be referring to critical thinking, physical, emotional, and life skills development, or they might mean the craft of the arts discipline they explored and the content of the art and subject areas they grasped. However, we will not know what they really mean until we help students build a metacognitive vocabulary to talk in depth about their learning through the arts.

In recent years, some schools in Oakland, California, have addressed these issues by using a strategy called Making Learning Visible. They use this framework to make visible the learning that is taking place every day in the classroom and make it the focus of the school community. Instead of Parent Nights, these schools present "Expositions of Learning." At these events, instead of bulletin boards consisting of the project title and the finished work, there are displays that document the learning process of an arts-integrated unit step by step, and quotes and reflections on the learning experience from students and teachers. Students, instead of "showing" what they have learned, actively "share" what they have learned in the classroom by teaching their parents and siblings an art process.

WHAT IS MAKING LEARNING VISIBLE?

Making Learning Visible is a learning framework developed by researchers at Project Zero at the Harvard Graduate School of Education, working collaboratively with educators at the Reggio Emilia school district in Italy. Project Zero researchers were interested in how the process of documentation at Reggio Emilia schools was crucial to the inquiry-based and group-oriented learning there and how these ideas could be used in U.S. schools. Oakland educators learned about this framework through local forums and projects presented by the Alameda County Office of Education, the Project Zero Summer Institute, and local lectures by visiting Reggio Emilia educators.

WHAT DOES MAKING LEARNING VISIBLE LOOK LIKE?

At a small charter school in Oakland, visual arts teacher Sara Stillman took pictures of her kindergarten students making art and later asked them to describe what they were thinking while they were making the art in the photograph. She transcribed their words under the photograph, and the students signed their names. This simple strategy created an opportunity for her students to develop a metacognitive language for their thinking process and revealed important information that Sara used to assess her student progress.

For example, one of the students described a photograph of herself painting by saying, "I was making squiggly lines. I got the idea to make squiggly lines from up in my head. The lines looked like the legs of an octopus." As someone who uses the Studio Habits of Mind (Hetland, Winner, Veenema, & Sheridan, 2007) to assess her student learning, Sara can see that her student is "envisioning" an image before she paints it and developing a metacognitve language to describe this skill. Sara can also see that once her student has put her idea on paper, she makes connections between her drawing and other objects in the world. In thought and image, Sara's student is caught in the act of building, through the practice of art, a very real bridge from her internal, mental world to the external world of physical reality and shared concepts.

By creating moments for her student to reflect on what she is thinking about what she is doing, Sara can track the student's bridge-building progress even as her pupil walks on the structure. In fact, the act of reflecting could aid students' bridge-building process, in part because "documentation is not limited to making visible what already exists; it also makes things exist precisely because it makes them visible and therefore possible" (Project Zero/Reggio Children, 2001, p. 17).

Another student described a photograph of himself making a group line painting with other children in this way: "All of the lines are different because they were made by different kids." Based on his reflection, we can see that he has created a theory for why all the lines on the paper are different, and it speaks to his beginning understanding that each person is capable of unique thoughts and unique ways of expressing them. Not only does he seem to understand each student as an autonomous creator, his neutral statement demonstrates an underlying tolerance for difference. Sara's student is developing a language about his personal learning as a participant within a learning group. His individual learning is extended by the simultaneous learning of his peers in a group context.

For an educator, these four sentences become a treasure trove of valuable information that helps assess what students are learning in the arts. Sara says, that Making Learning Visible strategies give her "an authentic reflection of that moment in time from my students' perspective. I find out what they understand and what they are learning."

These images were displayed in Sara's classroom year round, not just for the school's biannual Expositions of Learning. For students, the images reinforce the individual discoveries they have made and their developing metacognitive language. They also become a lexicon of learning, allowing each child to draw on the rich archive of learning by their peers. Because each student's learning is augmented by the learning of fellow students, Sara is creating a learning environment that can "foster relationships, loans of competencies, expectations, imitation and 'contagion'" (Project Zero/Reggio Children, 2001, p. 10).

This documentation also allowed Sara to share with the school community what her students were learning through the arts. A visitor could see the classroom in action even if the children were not present or engaged in arts learning. The text accompanying the image is crucial to the viewer's experience. Without the student voice, it would be tempting to make up our own story about what is happening in the picture. Instead, we read a play-by-play commentary that brings that moment of learning back to life.

Hatti Saunders and Opus Wilson, the third-grade team teachers at ASCEND School who also appear in Chapter 7, teach at a small school-by-design in Oakland. They create displays that document their arts-integrated units from beginning to end. These large process documentation panels begin as working documents in the classroom to chart students' day-to-day learning and then are displayed in the hallways for the biannual Exposition of Learning. Similar to Sara Stillman's pieces, this display includes photos and student quotations, but these elements are imbedded into a step-by-step description of the process, accompanied by examples of the work in progress, so that viewers can see the artwork and the associated learning take shape.

This display functions in multiple ways within the learning community. First, it serves as a working tool in the classroom. While constructing it, the students practice the vocabulary of the unit as they reflect on what they are learning.

Second, parents have an opportunity to see not only the finished work of the students but also each step of the multi-tiered project that involved drawing, expository writing, social studies, and musical composition. This display lays bare the rigorous learning process their children traversed, illuminates the complex intersections between the integrated subject areas, and provides a crash course on the content and skills involved so that parents can discuss the work with their children.

Third, the panels remake the school hallways into a text describing the collective story of learning. Instead of presenting disconnected artifacts of finished and

Figure 4.1. Making learning visible through student reflections.

"I noticed my partner's eyes are different sizes."

"I learned that eyelashes could be short or long."

"I noticed eyes have an oval shape."

"You can't trace the eye."

"You have to look at the eye to draw it."

"You gotta look real close and concentrate."

"Not all people's eyes are the same."

unrelated work from different classrooms and different subjects, this community story of learning is an inviting, ongoing, and developmental process. I have seen students in younger grades excitedly point out older siblings' work on the hallway walls to friends, who then stay as a group to read the road map of what they will likely do themselves when they progress to that next grade. Reciprocally, the public story provides an opportunity for older students to recognize the spiral relationships between the learning at different grade levels within the same subject area and to place themselves within this progressive story.

Fourth, the panels serve as a professional development tool. During the faculty meeting following the Exposition of Learning, teachers view the Making Learning Visible panels. They use a protocol that allows them to explore as a group what evidence of learning they see in the panel and to ask questions about the content and form of the display. Teachers new to Making Learning Visible experience firsthand how a teacher can use a documentation panel to communicate and assess the learning taking place in the classroom. For Hatti and Opus, it is an opportunity to hear their colleagues' feedback about their curriculum, collect suggestions from their peers, and explore the questions and new ideas generated by the conversation as they continue to refine their unit.

Inspired by the class displays at ASCEND School, Davina Katz Goldwasser, a seventh-grade teacher there, used Making Learning Visible on an individual student basis. She asked students to document their learning process during an immigration unit that included a play and to reflect on how they felt they learned best. Students created their own panels to make visible their own personal learning path through the immigration unit. One student depicted the path as a chronological and linear storyboard. Another depicted it as a radiating explosion from a central idea. The project provided Davina and viewers with a map for how students experienced the learning process and how they visualized it.

Reading the displays, a viewer could see how Davina's students were making connections to the material. While some students expressed amazement at historical information on immigration, others noted how the information dovetailed with migration stories told by parents. Although the displays focused on "how" students learned, the panels were also rich with information about "what" they learned, providing information about what knowledge they were most interested in or proud of learning.

The unit itself incorporated many pedagogical tools, including the study of books, lectures, group discussion, enactment of a historical play, and written reports. Despite the stereotype of lectures as "boring" and an outdated teaching mode, a large number of students noted that they learned best during lecture when they were able to listen and take notes. The displays also provided information about the arts-integrated component of the unit and created an opportunity to see how the students felt about the play they acted out and what they felt they learned in the process.

As these three examples across different grade levels, art forms, classroom situations, and academic disciplines illustrate, Making Learning Visible is effective in a variety of classrooms. Because Making Learning Visible is focused on the act of learning rather than on what is being learned, it can be used with a wide range of students and subject matter with success.

Figure 4.2. Detail from Making Learning Visible classroom display.

Photo by Carolyn S. Carr, Alameda County Office of Education Alliance for Arts Learning Leadership

FIRST STEPS TO MAKING YOUR STUDENT LEARNING VISIBLE

Some of these examples might be inspiring to you, but they also might seem a lot to undertake in your classroom or not appropriate, given your context. Or perhaps you don't know where to begin. If that is the case, try one of the following projects. Each should take about 15 minutes with materials you already have in your classroom. These ideas are presented as a sequence, but they can be tried individually as well.

1. Collect artifacts of the process, not just the final product. While finishing up a lesson, ask your students to choose an artifact that would best document an aspect of their learning that day. Maybe it is a paper plate paint palette, a draft of a script, a score with revisions on it, or a permission slip for a field trip to a museum. Ask students to write a brief caption describing how the artifact reflects their learning that day.

2. Guide a short reflective conversation with your students about their learning. Plan to take the time to stop the action in the classroom for the class to reflect. If you try this at the beginning of a lesson, you might ask students to reflect on the previous lesson and what they are most proud of learning thus far. If it is at the end of a lesson, you might ask your students when they felt challenged and what helped them overcome that challenge. Or if they could send themselves through a time machine to the day they started this project, what helpful understanding would they share with themselves? In other words, what do they understand now that they did not when they started?

When you have a reflective conversation with your students, it might be helpful to remember that students are used to being asked questions that have finite answers. A reflective conversation is quite different in that it encourages introspection and invites discussion of ideas that are unique to each student in the room. Let them know that there are no right or wrong answers to the questions you pose and underscore this with your responses. Also, keep in mind that the concept of "learning" is not easy for children. They know they are supposed to be doing "it," but the "it" is abstract and murky. This is partly because children are learning—taking in large amounts of new information, synthesizing it, and utilizing it—almost every waking minute.

Getting at the "learning" you are focusing on requires specific prompts to set the frame and a willingness to try follow-up questions if the first ones elicit answers that parrot your questions or reference whether they "liked it" or not. It might be helpful to students to scaffold the use of a metacognitive language while the learning is taking place. For example, you might say, "I see you are working together to think through your options and make a decision together." Or you might point out: "I notice many students are taking their time and contemplating how to draw what they envision in their mind." Having introduced these ideas in action, you can refer to these experiential examples later in your reflective conversation.

If a metacognitive vocabulary is new to your students, the first reflective conversation might be to build an age-appropriate thinking-word list to post in the classroom. For each word, ask students to give an example of how they experienced it that day. The list might include analyze, assume, brainstorm, choose, concentrate, consider, contemplate, find similarities or differences, focus, guess, imagine, interpret, make decisions, plan, question, recognize, reflect, revise, see relationships, synthesize, think, and understand.

3. Take time to reflect on your student learning. What stood out for you as a noteworthy moment today? Did you see a student have an *Aha!* moment? Did you notice a dynamic shift between students? Did the class as a whole take another step in an ongoing effort to master a skill or engage with an idea? Did you or your students encounter an unexpected challenge? What are your thoughts and questions about this?

Whether it is a moment of quiet reflection, an apportunity to jot down your thoughts on a scrap of paper, or a conversation with a fellow educator, take the time to reflect on the learning that is taking place in your classroom. Sometimes it is hard for us to take the time to reflect with so much competition for our time in the classroom. Remember, however, that you are the only person in the entire world of over 6 billion people who witnessed what you saw happen in your classroom. Your perspective as the teacher allows you a special vantage point that is critical to express, and simply by thinking it over, you move the learning in your classroom forward.

NEXT STEPS TO MAKING YOUR STUDENT LEARNING VISIBLE

If you have tried the first steps and are excited about continuing, here are some next steps to make your students' learning visible, directed to a specific purpose.

1. Create a question that can guide the reflective process. A question helps create a frame for the kind of learning you want to investigate and make visible. A good place to start is with questions for which "the answers are not obvious" and that "open up multiple points of view" (CAPE, 2007, p. 2).

I suggest focusing on a "burning question"—a question you have a strong desire to explore and understand. One burning question I have is, "What do my students think they are learning through the arts?" In the classroom, I ask, "What do we understand now that we didn't before we started?" This question creates an opportunity for students to reflect on their learning and how their understanding has changed during the project. It is a challenging question yet broad enough to capture perspectives across the spectrum. It is an opportunity not only for my students to share with me, but for me to share with them what I have learned. It is also a question that can be asked of our audience when we present our learning and our artwork.

2. Choose an upcoming opportunity to make your student learning visible. You might make your student learning visible as part of your everyday classroom practice, or part of a traditional public event, such as a Parent Night, exhibition, or concert. Or you might take advantage of a school newsletter, parent letter, Web site, bulletin board, or faculty meeting as a way to share. Most educators are already committed to communicating with the school community, so capitalize on what is already available to you. However, if your student learning lends itself to a new avenue or event, create the sharing opportunity that would be best.

3. Choose a form for your Making Learning Visible. The examples in this chapter are displays; there are many other options, including scrapbooks, slide shows, or blogs. Or students could keep individual or group journals with each page documenting questions they have and discoveries they make. A more experiential option could involve students' interviewing each other about what they discovered and then sharing what they learned from their partners with the class.

For public events featuring finished artwork, there are many ways to share your student learning. For example, in place of actor biographies, student reflections about what they learned during the process could be included in a program. At a performing arts showcase, students could perform poetry about their learning as interludes between longer pieces. At a mural dedication that honors the gift from the student artists to the school, students could also share the gift of learning they experienced while creating the mural. For more ideas, check out the Making Learning Visible Toolkit online (Alameda County Office of Education, no date). Whatever form you choose, remember that it is an opportunity for you as the emcee to share with your community what you feel is most important about what your students learned.

4. Keep the focus on learning. As you and your students work together to make their learning visible, continually check in about how the learning itself and not simply the activities of the classroom are being made visible. Students recounting the steps of the process of how they made a mural versus students recounting their thinking and how it changed over the course of making a mural are two related yet different stories. Key questions to keep in mind are, What do my students think about what they are doing and learning, and What do I think about what my students are learning?

Engage with the Making Learning Visible piece again and again with your students. Treat it as a work in progress and use it as a way to continue a reflective conversation with students. Don't be surprised if each time you engage with it, you and your students discover that some significant aspect of their learning is missing from the story. This discovery is a sign that the Making Learning Visible process is working. It is doing its job of bringing to light the multiple facets of learning so that you can work together to figure out how best to share them.

5. Find a Making Learning Visible partner. Introduce a like-minded colleague to these ideas and invite him or her to try Making Learning Visible with his or her students. Together you will be able to brainstorm with a shared knowledge of your context. You will have a ready listener with whom to share your teacher reflections. You will be able to consult with each other during the process and give each other feedback on results in the classroom. Making Learning Visible shifts the focus from product to process, from logistics to learning, and from doing to reflecting; having a partner at your side while you traverse this exciting territory will be very helpful.

IS IT WORKING?

As you engage with the Making Learning Visible process, you might wonder, How do I know if this is working? Ask yourself the following questions. The answers will help sharpen the focus of your investigation into learning to yield the most helpful information to you and your students.

What Did I Learn About
- Individual students and their learning processes or my class as a learning community?
- My lesson plan or the subject matter/discipline we are learning about?
- The process of learning through the arts?
- The question or idea that inspired the Making Learning Visible piece?

Did My Students Have an Opportunity to
- Engage with their individual or group learning process?
- Develop a vocabulary for metacognitive thinking and what it means to them?
- Reflect thoughtfully on their learning experience and express their feelings, discoveries, and questions to their learning community?
- Hear about and engage with the learning process of their peers?
- Value their own learning as much as their completed work?
- Affect the learning culture in the classroom?

What Did Viewers of Our Making Learning Visible Project Learn About
- Individual students or the class and their learning experience?
- The subject matter or discipline we are learning about?

- The process of learning through the arts?
- The question or idea that inspired the Making Learning Visible piece?

This type of reflection will help draw out what steps you might take next with the Making Learning Visible process and with your teaching.

THE BEAUTY OF MAKING LEARNING VISIBLE

Making Learning Visible can be effective at every age level in every arts discipline and academic subject matter, and for each member of the learning community in multiple ways. The beauty of Making Learning Visible is that it simply takes the learning that is happening in the classroom and makes it accessible. Once it is made available to everyone, it enhances the experience for both students and teachers. It demonstrates that everyone's ideas are important and encourages students to take pride in what they are learning.

Making Learning Visible is a perfect strategy for my vision of the ideal Parent Night. It would actually be Parent Day—it would happen during the school day—and nothing unusual would be arranged. Parents would be invited to join the class and participate, to the degree they feel comfortable, in the real learning that happens every day in the classroom. Parents would watch and listen to the ongoing metacognitive conversation between teacher and students about the learning taking place before them. Students would guide their parents through displays and experiences to share their learning further. As their children move through the grades and encounter different arts disciplines, parents alongside their children would develop a sophisticated language to express the learning process. Ultimately, everyone would have a common language to honor the students and what they have learned.

REFERENCES

Alameda County Office of Education. (no date). *Making Learning Visible Toolkit*. Retrieved July 1, 2009, from http://www.artiseducation.org/downloads/MakingLearningVisible Toolkit.pdf

CAPE (Chicago Arts Partnerships in Education). (2007). *How to develop good questions in inquiry based education*. Retrieved March 5, 2010, from http://capeweb.org/wp-content/uploads/2010/06/good-questions.pdf

Hetland, L., Winner, E., Veenema, S., & Sheridan, K. (2007). *Studio thinking: The real benefits of arts education*. New York: Teachers College Press.

Project Zero/Reggio Children. (2001). *Making learning visible: Children as individual and group learners*. Reggio Emilia, Italy: Reggio Children.

PART III

Art in Every School

CHAPTER 5

Leadership for and in the Arts

Lynda Tredway and Rebecca Wheat

IMAGINE A SCHOOL with a dancer, musicians, and other specialists devoted to the visual and performing arts—a school where artists worked closely with classroom teachers, where staff members enjoyed teaching, and where families selected the school. This was Arts Magnet School in Berkeley, California, in 1986, when Rebecca was the school's principal. The school became so popular that eventually the school district had to institute a lottery process to select students. The school went on to win the first California Distinguished School Award for Berkeley Unified School District based on the school's passionate belief that the arts are a crucial component of an educated individual (Eisner, 2004; Greene, 1991; McCarthy, Ondaatje, Zakaras, & Brooks, 2005; Stevenson, 2006). The school delivered a high-quality arts program to children, paying attention to literacy and numeracy without sacrificing any part of the development of the whole child (Bresler, 2005; Davis, 2005; West, 2000; Witherall, 2000).

Arts Magnet School demonstrated what could become a reality when commitment, hard work, and love of the arts all come together with a belief that the arts are central to holistic learning (Eisner, 2005a, 2005b; McCarthy et al., 2005). The leader's advocacy was the cornerstone of the implementation because the leader, in collaboration with teachers, staff, and community, carried and protected this vision: The arts, when thoughtfully integrated, can be a catalyst for change at a school and success for students in many of the life skills critical for their development and eventual success in school and beyond (McCarthy et al., 2005; Stevenson, 2006).

Today, faced with the external accountability mandates, the arts in many districts and schools have taken a backseat to testing and several hours a day devoted to literacy drills or interventions for students who are not at the proficient level. Some schools have temporarily abandoned arts in the curriculum to concentrate on literacy and numeracy, filling up the elementary day with 2.5 hours of reading, and intervention classes taking the place of arts periods in middle and high school. Other schools struggle to incorporate the arts (Cockburn, 1991; Gallas, 1991; Hetland, Winner, Veenema, & Sheridan, 2007; Ross, 2005; Siegesmund, 2005).

Despite these scenarios, courageous educators keep the flame of arts education burning. We interviewed three administrators: Matin Abdel-Qawi, principal of East Oakland School of the Arts; Karling Aguilera-Fort, former principal of San Francisco's Fairmont Elementary School and now assistant superintendent of the San Francisco Unified School District; and Larissa Adam, principal of ASCEND School in Oakland. All three are graduates of the Principal Leadership Institute at the University of California, Berkeley, and are successfully integrating the arts in three public urban California schools. In this chapter, they share insights on how administrators can keep the arts in school as a core part of the curriculum.

The work and actions of these administrators give us all hope about what can happen, given a fundamental belief that a thriving arts focus can help drive reform and achievement in schools. Children and young people need the arts—for their cognitive development, for lessons about perseverance and resilience, for building the belief that effort is an important attribute of success in any endeavor (Weiner, 1994).

LESSONS LEARNED

From talking to these three administrators, we have developed a set of criteria—or lessons learned—that offer direction to other leaders who are building or maintaining an arts focus. Some lessons are central to the arts pulse of a school, and others are smaller; all are important. These lessons are critical to keeping art at the center of effective teaching and learning, although on the surface, they appear self-evident. However, because embedding and supporting the arts systematically in elementary, middle, and high schools seems to keep slipping through our fingers, the lessons gathered from the experiences of the three leaders bear repetition and reinforcement.

LESSON ONE: THE LEADER SETS THE TONE

All three leaders truly believe that the arts are critically important to the whole child and whole school. Matin Abdel-Qawi, principal of East Oakland School of the Arts (EOSA), a small school begun in 2004, explains this view: "[It] starts with the commitment to the arts. It starts with that. So if you're unconditionally committed to the arts and sincerely believe that the arts can play a significant role in developing children to be whole, positive, productive citizens—then if you start with that premise, then you just work from there." Through the small-schools movement in Oakland, which began in the late 1990s, multiple schools, including EOSA, have been able to support from their inception the development of leaders and schools committed to the arts.

This same commitment is expressed somewhat differently by Karling Aguilera-Fort, former principal of Fairmount Elementary School in San Francisco and now assistant superintendent in the San Francisco Unified School District

(SFUSD). He says, "The first [principle] concerning the arts comes from my own belief that as a human being we need something that will enrich our life; that will provide us a different perspective of the world outside. Then, to back it up—I have to do it—I look at all this research that shows that if students are immersed in art, and given the possibility of using art and receiving art, they are more creative." This confirms what we know from the literature about the value of arts in the human experience and in the learning environment (Eisner, 2004, 2005a, 2005b; Fiske, 1999; Greene, 1991; Noddings, 2005).

Finally, principal Larissa Adam of ASCEND, a K–8 small school in Oakland, California, comments, "I think particularly as our kids get older and reach adolescence and they're feeling a lot more pressure outside of the school . . . [that] the arts keep them hooked in." The adolescent-brain research underscores the importance of the arts as exploratory at middle school for the social, emotional, and intellectual development of the adolescent brain and students' ability to navigate a difficult stage of life and remain resilient (California Department of Education, 2009; Sylwester, 1995).

It is this intense personal commitment to and ongoing administrative support of the arts by the principal that sets a tone and spirit that says that the arts are critical to the school. As reiterated in the leadership literature concerning the necessary vision of the leader and his or her role in creating a coherent and cohesive school, a leader who respects and has passion for the arts as a part of his or her vision of the school is essential if the arts are to flourish (Senge, Cambron-McCabe, Lucas, Smith, Dutton, & Klenier, 2000).

LESSON TWO: STARTING SMALL IS FINE

It is fine to start small and expand. "Begin somewhere," comments Abdel-Qawi. He says, "Start small. Offer one section of spoken word. Offer one section of drama. Have an artist in residence. Find $7,000 or $8,000 that will allow one person to come in once a week for the whole school year to work with 20 kids. Just start off with that, if that's all you can do." The "tipping-point theory" applies here (Gladwell, 2002). Success in the arts does not require a full-scale beginning; a small, but successful, effort demonstrates to others the possibility and gives the leader and teachers a chance to fine-tune the work before it becomes too large. Pilot efforts pay off. The rule of thumb is to choose something carefully, implement it systematically, and keep it up and running until there is either more interest or more money.

A starting place at Fairmount School was ballroom dancing. Comments Principal Aguilera-Fort, "We are the first school in San Francisco Unified to ever have ballroom dancing. And now other schools are following our path. And the whole idea came after we watched a documentary about ballroom dancing in New York City public schools [Agrelo, 2005]. I saw it and I just said, 'We have to do something similar. Why can't we do this?' I came back to school. I spoke with the PTA people and some of them watched the documentary. We left the conversation right there. December we have our big event for the holidays, and at the end I asked to dance with another teacher on the stage, and of course the kids and the parents [and] the principal [were] dancing; everyone [was] clapping." A deep moral commitment and a leader's examples can actually affect the change process at a school if the leader is willing to commit to a "sighting" and engage the school community in the change process collaboratively (McDonald, 1996; DuFour, Dufour, Eaker, & Many, 2006). A sighting is "a rare glimpse of values operating below the surface of espoused belief, an empirical test of what really counts in a particular school" (McDonald, 1996, p. 23). It offers an opportunity to match one's beliefs with behaviors and policies that animate schools.

Starting with one area lets the administrator take a careful look at the instructional minutes required to integrate the arts and be creative about using some arts workshops as physical education or required arts minutes. Secondary schools have instituted dance as a physical education class; since students have to have PE "minutes," this is an alternative solution.

LESSON THREE: BRING TEACHING STAFF AND ARTISTS TOGETHER

How staff works with professionals is an important part of the arts program. The optimum model is when teachers and artists plan together. Larissa Adam comments, "We have on staff two visual arts coaches, both part time, and a part-time musical arts-integration coach, who meet one on one or in pairs with classroom teachers and together they plan how to integrate the arts, both visual and music, into the instruction of language arts, science, history, and mathematics through semester or yearlong learning."

Aguilera-Fort weighs in: "The students are receiving three types of art programs; one class is receiving ballet *folklorico*—Mexican dance. The other one is receiving performing arts—drama, poetry. And the other one is doing visual art and science integrated." The consultants (teaching artists) are hired to work with students, but teachers observe; once teachers have seen the way artists work, they learn how to be more fluid in their pedagogical approaches, building the arts into their instructional programs (Dobbs, 1993). For example, instead of the students' walking in lines to an activity or lunch, the teachers might ask them to practice the dance movements they have learned, or the teacher begins to see the importance of kinesthetics for learning in other areas. Indeed, once teachers have observed student success in the arts, they also have a different sense of how capable and engaged students are.

Schools have to experiment with different models and schedules, depending on their school's structure, resources, schedules, and artist availability. Contextualizing the artistic work in each school site is critical, but paying attention to these criteria for working with artists is useful: Teachers should observe how the artists work and have time to reflect about how to incorporate the arts in all content areas.

LESSON FOUR: FORM PARTNERSHIPS TO KEEP YOUR COMMUNITY WORKING WITH YOU

The administrators interviewed for this chapter know how important it is to keep their community—the parents and the community organizations—working with them to support arts and arts integration. According to Aguilera-Fort, "The programs cannot be decided by one person. So if the community—most of the parents—feel that they do want dancing, then you have to really look at what the community wants." Keeping your community involved, informed, and excited about your arts program is imperative for long-term success.

Forming partnerships with other arts organizations is vital and sets the tone for success. Adam, the principal of ASCEND School, comments, "So the county office [of education] connected us into a very big grant that placed artists in residence at our school. For the first year every single core teacher was partnered with a musician and a visual artist who worked with us for about 2 hours a week. The following year the grant was cut in half by the state and so that went down to every other week. And then the following year after that they cut the funding completely. At that point, though, we had had 2 years of amazing experiences with using the arts as an equity tool, using the arts to increase students' understanding of subject matter, but also using the arts as a tool to help them express their learning in multiple ways." The use of a grant is the germ of an idea that can then become a part of the way the institution operates. The principal continues, "If we did not have partners who were experts in the arts and experts in music we could not have done this—because we would not have had quality programs. We have a lot of expertise in language arts and math and science and history—but we are not professional artists." Arts organizations are good partners because they bring the knowledge, will, skill, and dispositions to the work, helping the school leader and teachers maintain focus.

The importance of partnering with organizations is reiterated by the late Denise Brown, former vice principal of Arts and Humanities Academy, a small school at Berkeley High. "Probably our biggest connection was [the] Alameda County [Office of Education]. That connection really helped propel us. It was able to get us professional development, arts integration, and curriculum mapping." This connection provided the support to look at the various parts of arts integration that needed to occur simultaneously if the program was to become institutionalized: Teachers needed professional development, including experiences in the arts, and the current curriculum needed to be integrated with the arts to magnify its impact.

Administrators are urged to look in their own communities and see what organizations are willing to partner. Often a county office of education has excellent resources and ideas. Many times, small arts organization provide an opportunity to work with schools in collaborative and supportive ways. At times grants or matching funds are available to enhance this process. Schools are urged to "think outside the box" in terms of funding sources or partnerships when seeking various arts partners. Arts and artists are often willing to customize their school involvement. Initially, this takes time, but once the processes have been set up in the initial year of implementation, the project and artist connections become easier. Thus the first step of forming partnership is the most time consuming, but the long-term payoff, as seen in Lesson Five, in terms of student and teacher experiences and learning, is well worth the initial effort.

LESSON FIVE: ENGAGEMENT PAYS OFF

While we have emphasized some ways that school leaders can enhance the arts, we would be remiss if we did not discuss the payoff these administrators see when arts are included in their schools. East Oakland School of the Arts is one of three small schools carved out of Castlemont High, a large comprehensive public high school, in 2007. Abdel-Qawi was an assistant principal at the former Castlemont and helped to plan the conversion. He had no formal arts background; however, his beliefs about the arts were based on his experience of seeing how students who had deep and regular arts experiences were connected to school. Comments Abdel-Qawi, "It is an amazing accomplishment, considering that at the old Castlemont we never had more than 100 people [from the community at a school event] out of 1,500 or 1,600 [families at the school]. Our relationship with the community and our families is much better than it has ever been. So we had a wonderful event and hundreds of people there participating. So we know that it's improving; we know that it's a result of what we've done in this short time that our parents are getting more engaged."

Larissa Adam says, "We see quite a difference. We have kids who have been here and have been a part of the program for several years who have been immersed in the arts and inquiry learning because that's what their learning exhibitions [summative assessments] are about. We have students [who] are expressing their learning in multiple ways and not being afraid to do so. So they're risk takers academically." The risk-taking leads to success, which in turn leads to students being able to attribute their success to their effort, which typically leads to more effort and intellectual development (Ross, 2005). As Aguilera-Fort says, "They are 9, 10, 11—and they are amazing. They are looking forward to every single lesson. Everyone knows about the ballroom dancing about the school. Because we are doing it [we had] the press and the media [at the school]. And now everyone sees that it's working and we are bringing that ballroom dancing into the school day."

FROM LESSONS LEARNED TO LEADERSHIP FOR THE ARTS

Children educated in the arts are enriched for life, as are families exposed to the arts. Administrators offer ideas, perspective, hope, and inspiration. Their vision and active participation are essential elements for arts integration. In this age of accountability focused on standardized testing, it is possible—and even necessary—to include arts in the curriculum. One can start small and build on each success. The payoffs are great: engaged children and families who truly know the arts are critical to educating fully our young people.

REFERENCES

Agrelo, M. (Director). (2005). *Mad hot ballroom* [Motion picture]. United States: Paramount.

Bresler, L. (2005). Music and the intellect: Perspectives, interpretations, and implications for education. *Phi Delta Kappan, 87*(1), 24–31.

California Department of Education. (2009). *Taking Center Stage II.* Retrieved April 20, 2009, from http://pubs.cde.ca.gov/tcsii/ch4/adolescentneeds.aspx

Cockburn, V. (1991). The uses of folk music and songwriting in the classroom. *Harvard Educational Review, 61*(1), 71–79.

Davis, J. H. (2005). Redefining Ratso Rizzo: Learning from the arts about process and reflection. *Phi Delta Kappan, 87*(1), 11–17.

Dobbs, S. M. (2003). *Learning in and through art: A guide to discipline-based art education.* Los Angeles: J. Paul Getty Foundation.

DuFour, R., DuFour, R., Eaker, R., & Many, T. (2006). *Learning by doing: A handbook for professional learning communities at work.* Bloomington, IN: Solution Tree.

Eisner, E. (2004). *The arts and the creation of mind.* New Haven, CT: Yale University Press.

Eisner, E. (2005a). Back to whole. *Educational Leadership, 63*(1), 14–19.

Eisner, E. (2005b). Opening a shuttered window: An introduction to a special section on the arts and the intellect. *Phi Delta Kappan, 87*(1), 8–10.

Fiske, E., (Ed.) (1999). *Champions of change: The impact of the arts on learning.* Washington, DC: Arts Education Partnership.

Gallas, K. (1991). Art as epistemology: Enabling children to know what they know. *Harvard Educational Review, 61*(1), 40–50.

Gladwell, M. (2002). *The tipping point: How little things can make a big difference.* Boston: Little, Brown.

Greene, M. (1991). Texts and margins. *Harvard Educational Review, 61*(1), 27–39.

Hetland, L., Winner, E., Veenema, S., & Sheridan, K. (2007). *Studio thinking: The real benefits of visual arts education.* New York: Teachers College.

McCarthy, K. F., Ondaatje, E. H., Zakaras, L., & Brooks, A. (2005). *Gifts of the muse: Reframing the debate about the benefits of the arts.* Santa Monica, CA: Rand.

McDonald, J. P. (1996). *Redesigning school: Lessons for the 21st century.* San Francisco: Jossey Bass.

Noddings, N. (2005). What does it mean to educate the whole child? *Educational Leadership, 63*(1), 8–13.

Ross, J. (2005). A hidden soul of artistry: Thinking in forgotten areas of the arts. *Phi Delta Kappan, 87*(1), 32–37.

Senge, P., Cambron-McCabe, N., Lucas, T., Smith, B., Dutton, J., & Klenier, A. (2000). *Schools that learn: A fifth discipline fieldbook for educators, parents, and everyone who cares about education.* New York: Doubleday Dell.

Siegesmund, R. (2005). Teaching qualitative reasoning: portraits of practice. *Phi Delta Kappan, 87*(1), 18–23.

Stevenson, L. M. (2006). The arts: Possibilities for teaching and learning. *Principal's Research Review, 1*(2), 1–6.

Sylwester, R. (1995). *A celebration of neurons: An educator's guide to the human brain.* Alexandria, VA: Association for Supervision and Curriculum Development.

Weiner, B. (1994). Ability versus effort revisited: The moral determinants of achievement evaluation and achievement as a moral system. *Educational Psychologist, 29*(3), 163–172.

West, D. (2000, Summer). An arts education: A necessary component to building the whole child. *Educational Horizons, 78*(4), 176–178.

Witherall, N. (2000, Summer). Promoting understanding: Teaching literacy through the arts. *Educational Horizons*, 179–183.

CHAPTER 6

Arts Integration

One School, One Step at a Time

Debra Koppman

THIS IS THE story of how Sequoia Elementary, a public school in Oakland, California, developed a visual arts program that led to arts integration across the curriculum over a period of 12 years. I tell this story, in part, because I am so proud of what has been accomplished at Sequoia, but also because the story has lessons for teachers, artists, and administrators at other schools. The changes at Sequoia have not been easy, and I convey the complications and struggles we faced as well as the benefits of creating a model environment for schoolwide arts integration. My hope is this story will inspire others to establish arts programs and integrate the arts across the curriculum. I also hope it will prepare others to take advantage of every opportunity and prepare for the inevitable hitches along the way. As you read this chapter, think about where your own school is in establishing the arts as a priority and a tool for learning in many subject areas. At each step, I present the ups and downs and share the lessons we have learned so you can reflect on how to further your own work.

STEP 1: YOU GOTTA HAVE ART TO START!

Initially my involvement at Sequoia Elementary developed simply out of a need for one kind of arts integration in my own life. As an artist, an educator, and the mama of a small child, I was commuting to several part-time college teaching jobs and juggling day care and studio time. I wanted to integrate my skills into useful community work, be with my child, and make art. When my daughter was 2 years old, my family went to Lima, Peru, where my husband and I had Fulbright teaching fellowships. There, I was inspired by a beautiful puppet theater on a simple stage in a public park. The puppets and the productions were actually very sophisticated and I was drawn to the idea that perhaps I could teach myself how to make some kind of puppets and then teach this to kids, who could then use puppets to perform plays.

On my return, I found a book on teaching puppetry to kids. One line stood out. It suggested taking an entire classroom out on the street for a parade with their puppets. At this point, I had no experience teaching children, and my own sculpture was totally nonrepresentational. But I thought if I could build dramatic puppets, and from there get the school community excited about my idea for plays, and a schoolwide parade, maybe I could get some funding.

From the very beginning of this project in 1998, I had a vague concept of arts integration without exactly using this language. It seemed natural to me that we could create something visual, which could be inspired by and in turn inspire writing, and later culminate in performance. As it turned out, this kind of project, promising curriculum ties to language arts and social studies, got funded by the California Arts Council and subsequently by the City of Oakland. After many years when schools cut art because funding disappeared and it was no longer considered "basic," Sequoia had an arts program.

Arts integration is a phrase open to multiple interpretations, most of them rich with possibilities for understanding the importance of the arts in educating children. In schools with no arts, however, just getting art in the school, as a dedicated subject area with a dedicated time slot, provides a starting point toward potential integration of arts and other subjects. This is where we started at Sequoia, with the artist-in-residence model provided for many years by the California Arts Council. Using this model, an artist visits classrooms to instruct children, and the classroom teachers are always present with the artist, so they can benefit from arts instruction while supporting the artist's work with the students.

While having an art program does not suggest *arts integration*, it is a crucial first step. Implementing arts integration at the schoolwide level without arts training for students and teachers provides little to work with.

Integrating the arts into the life of the school was our first step toward eventual arts integration in the curriculum. We wanted the whole school community to value visual art as one vital aspect of the school's curriculum. We wanted the arts to become part of the school's consciousness and identity. The idea of a parade with all the children and their puppets captured the imagination of the school principal and allowed me and the arts program entry into the school. At the end of our 1st year creating the arts program, we held that parade. It connected and integrated the students and their work with the larger community and functioned as guerrilla advertising for public education. The arts were also a leveler between children, creating a larger space in which to see all the children as "gifted" in some way. Access to the arts, as an integrated component of the school culture, therefore became a means toward equity, offering expanded learning opportunities and alternative means to shine.

From the beginning I also had a more subversive vision of a school that would eventually embrace the arts, not just as one isolated subject area, but as a pathway to learning in multiple subject areas, including social studies, science, language arts, and performance. A larger and related fantasy has been the idea that the entire city of Oakland would embrace arts-based education to take advantage of the city's wealth of artistic talent, while helping to revitalize and reform our city's schools. "Imagine a school system," I have thought, "where artists working in every one of our public schools are helping teachers to develop performances, sets, book arts, dances, and murals. Imagine these schools teeming with enthusiastic and engaged children, learning through hands-on, experiential curriculum. Watch as those previously public school–averse families clamor for a place for their children in Oakland's public schools."

Through 12 years of continued funding, professional development, and an evolving understanding of arts integration, Sequoia has moved from having only a stand-alone arts program to a more sustainable and complex level of arts integration. Putting an arts program in place, as we did that 1st year, is possible fairly quickly with energetic and capable artists and teachers and a reasonable level of institutional and economic support. Arts integration, in which a sustainable and independent arts program is maintained, while simultaneously creating arts-integrated classroom curriculum infused with arts learning, is much more complicated, taking enormous time, energy, will, intention, leadership, and funding, as the following years illustrated. We are still engaged in this task and see it as ongoing.

STEP 2: PUPPETS ALIVE! AT SEQUOIA ELEMENTARY

School and community support for the arts at Sequoia began with the Puppets Alive! project. For 3 years, each child planned, created, painted, and decorated his

Figure 6.1. *Puppets Alive!* **Sequoia Elementary School.**

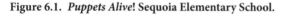

Photo by Debra Koppman.

or her own large-scale papier-mâché puppet from recycled materials. From things that other people threw away, magical creatures appeared.

The children used PVC pipes, paper plates, cardboard, newspaper, foam, paper towel rolls, and other recyclable materials and learned to turn these into fanciful tropical fish, winged creatures, desert and jungle animals, fairies, elves, princesses, elephant queens, witches, and many other characters culled from stories or invented as part of the process. Teachers used folktales from around the world as the broad conceptual framework and emphasized cultural diversity and cross-cultural understanding to prompt these varied puppet characters and student-written performance projects. The puppets stood as concrete models of children's abilities to function as artist-inventors and their own capacity to learn, grow, and imagine. Each of these puppets became an essential character in a play that required the efforts, cooperation, and voices of the entire cast. The plays were performed in schoolwide assemblies and neighborhood venues, including the local public library, a nearby senior citizens home, and the Oakland Museum. At the end of each of those first 3 years all 350 children, with their puppets, paraded out of the schoolyard and into the streets of the community.

Puppets Alive! taught individual creativity, group collaboration, and community development simultaneously and continuously. Children developed their own special project, and as a class, their individual work came together, part of something that no individual could create on his or her own. Shared with parents, neighbors, and the world outside the school, the group projects embodied the creative energy of the school community of which each child was a part.

Initially there was no dedicated art room, so I went around from class to class with my cart, buckets of water, and large blue plastic tarps, managing to somehow stain the floors of every single classroom. The 1st year the school was also in the process of modernization, so many of the classrooms were in temporary portables, which were even more cramped than ordinary classrooms.

I didn't know anything about child development or grade-level appropriateness. I assumed that everyone from kindergarten through fifth grade would be able to do something with the materials and the instruction I was offering. This clearly had mixed results, particularly at the level of kindergarten. However, in every class, including two kindergarten classrooms, children created positive and surprising things—perhaps because I didn't quite realize that the work was much too sophisticated for some of the students. Over the course of many years, I have got better at adapting what I am doing for various grade levels, but I have very mixed feelings about this. Not knowing anything about students' limitations led me to challenge them toward magnificent accomplishments.

Seeing the students' creations sustained me the first years. You could not walk into the school and miss these large-scale stick puppets. Most of them were at least three feet tall, with lots of long protrusions such as elephant trunks, tails, horns, or wildly curled hair. While they were in process, they were standing in buckets of sand in the classrooms and halls. When they were finished, they lived in the hallways, on stands built out of PVC tubes by the Dads' Club. The puppets got more and more sophisticated over the course of 3 years, as the children became more confident with the materials; their sculpture skills; and the level of detail they could lend to painting, pattern, and decoration. At some point, we were also adding parts, such as tails and legs, which could gently move. We were often pushing the limits of what could actually hold together with papier-mâché, as we had birds with enormous wing spans, seemingly endless snake bodies, deer horns going on forever, elephant trunks that could knock out a preschooler, and rabbit ears much longer than you've ever seen.

On the plus side, all this created a lot of enthusiasm for art and an incredible visual impact. As 350 children holding puppets above their heads marched out onto the street, they gave visual proof of their abilities to create over a sustained period of time something they had never seen before. The parade provided a way to see all these children as clever and creative, in total opposition to the prevailing gloomy, low-testing, underachieving stereotype of Oakland public school children in the media.

Even at the beginning, we saw the possibility for integrating the arts in other curricular areas. Performances connected the puppets to learning spoken and written language. For the most part, teachers supported the puppet project with a great deal of spirit, seeing it as a positive learning opportunity for their students. Many modified or adapted existing folktales or put together scripts based on poetry or myths to engage students in writing.

Puppets Alive! had its rocky moments, too. From the outset, the performances required a huge amount of time and effort on the part of classroom teachers, apart from the time that had already been set aside for visual art. Time became more problematic each year. Although the performances themselves were beautiful, and always better than teachers initially imagined, the rising levels of anxiety for teachers was high. By the 3rd year of this project, time constraints from testing and a new reading program made rehearsing stressful and untenable. By the end of the 3rd year, teachers were begging to let go of the performances. At this point, we had another problem. The outrageous and beautiful creatures enlivening our hallways turned out to be in violation of fire codes. So we made changes to the project, dropping the performances and enormous papier-mâché puppets, while still holding the year-end parade with smaller papier-mâché masks.

This original project was successful in many ways. It immediately and dramatically garnered support for maintaining an art program at the school. Because the puppets and the parade were visually compelling, we enjoyed attention in the press and received funding from a variety of sources. The puppet project was a great way to get an art program established and plant the seeds for arts integration. However, it required an enormous amount of blind faith, boundless energy, willing faculty, and flexibility on everyone's part. It also needed to grow and change and adapt with the changing needs of the school.

If you are thinking of launching an arts program at your school, Puppets Alive! provides some lessons. First, find a specialized arts provider so classroom teachers are supported and can learn to use art materials and processes on their own. Second, to sustain this kind of schoolwide project, enlist the administration as well as artists and teachers to develop a vision of why and how such a project contributes to and amplifies the goals for student learning at your school. Third, start early to find reliable, ongoing funding, which is at the present eternally problematic and inherently inequitable. Puppets Alive! was originally funded by the California Arts Council and the City of Oakland. In our case, funders appreciated that we were explicit about the connection between the arts and multicultural literature and therefore core classroom curriculum. They also appreciated that the project was arts-based, not arts-enriched education, meaning art, in addition to being a subject itself, was directly connected to and furthered learning across the disciplines. The project was not an add-on or enrichment only for students in after-school or gifted and talented programs. The project served all students at the school. Making these connections requires time for teachers to plan. Finally, collaborate. Various community arts organizations collaborated with Sequoia over the years. For several years, we had students from Oakland High School's Visual Arts Magnet Program, who worked as mentors to our children. The East Bay Community Foundation helped us fund a choreographer and a jazz poet for one school year, Stagebridge supported us with a storyteller, and Artship functioned for many years as the fiscal agent and community advocate.

Because until recently schools have had no guaranteed, reliable funding for arts programs, luck, chance, and the politics of grant writing have determined which projects get funded at particular schools. Those of us writing the grants promise incredible outcomes for little money. This is obviously appealing to funders, but ultimately brings consequences for sustainability that administrators, teachers, and artists need to consider. Everyone wants to create dynamic, educationally valuable arts programs. At Sequoia we continue to modify the design of our program, holding on to its original spirit and integrity, while trying to function in the world of actual time and resources. It's not easy, but we are proof it can be done!

STEP 3: CONSTANTLY CHANGING AND MOVING TOWARD INTEGRATION

Change is hard but also inevitable. The arts program at Sequoia had to change to meet fluctuating levels of funding, time demands, and fire codes. When funding diminished and disappeared, we never abandoned the arts program. Instead, we changed focus and activities. When funding reappeared, we continued to reinvent the Sequoia arts program. Such reinvention kept the program vital and responsive to the needs of the school.

We decided to turn roadblocks into opportunities. We needed to drop the obligatory puppet performances, and we had no way to store large-scale puppets.

We wanted kids to have art class on an ongoing and frequent basis, instead of the one large stretch of time each class got for the puppet project. We wanted to maintain the tradition of the Sequoia parade, for its concept of schoolwide community and neighborhood outreach. We came to think of masks as something that also could be paraded, could be done within the constraints of the existing grants, could be hung up rather than built on poles, and maintained the possibility for inspiring writing projects and plays.

After several years focused exclusively on puppets, we changed the frame and the title of the school's arts project to "Telling Our Stories." The title was open enough to hold our parade, to provide our students with arts experiences in different choices of media, and to allow for new and varied ways to connect to language arts curriculum. We divided the year into modules, "Honoring Our Ancestors," "Telling Our Stories," and "Re-creating Ourselves," and incorporated small-scale puppets, masks, bookmaking, printmaking, drawing, and painting.

"Honoring Our Ancestors" grew from work teachers were already doing. Each fall several classes studied the Day of the Dead and set up a collective "Memory Table" with photographs and memorabilia in the school lobby. This provided a starting point for creating art—salt dough puppets in honor of the ancestors to understand personal and collective history—and making literacy connections by engaging in interviews with family members, drafting letters, and writing poetry. For several years, we invited these puppets to an expanded community Memory Table displayed in the school lobby. We included banners decorated with drawings of these puppets and imagined advice from the ancestors, and we followed up by writing letters; poems; and in some cases, books about personal stories, family

Figure 6.2. Day of the Dead Memory Table, Sequoia Elementary School.

Photo by Debra Koppman.

history, and cultural heritage, drawing on the Bay Area Writing Project's "Where I'm From" curriculum. We were honored to be invited to display our fifth graders' "Honoring Our Ancestors" project as part of the Oakland Museum's Day of the Dead celebration.

"Telling Our Stories" was generally tied in some way to bookmaking. Some years this unit involved drawing self-portraits, which led to creating moveable self-portrait puppets, or making salt dough ancestors for theater storybooks called "Conversations with My Ancestor." Some years "Telling Our Stories" was more specifically tied to writing projects in the classrooms, with the children designing and illustrating various kinds of books, some of which also corresponded to units in the district's reading program. One year, teachers incorporated the books into an evening literacy event, displaying them for the parents and children who returned to school in their pajamas for story time. The children also shared the books with each other in buddy classes.

"Re-creating Ourselves" was also open enough to be varied, but generally tied to creating fairly large-scale cast plaster or papier-mâché masks, intended as focal points for the children to imagine either their alter egos or their protector spirits, again as a prompt for writing. Recently, we completed a self-portrait drawing project with all the children. These drawings were exhibited at the Alameda County Office of Education and selected for that year's promotional Art Is Education! poster. I thought we could sneak in one extra project and have each child create another self-portrait using acrylic on panel. These would be mounted like an enormous quilt, forming a pieced-together mural. I realized, however, that an extra project does not just get sneaked in, and that I was underestimating the amount of effort, time, and learning needed. We had time to paint the portraits or make the alter ego and protector spirit masks, but not both. At that point, drawing and painting self-portraits was more connected than building masks to the work we had done over the course of the year. We dropped the masks and discontinued the parade. Although it was hard to let go of the Sequoia School Parade, an ongoing 7-year neighborhood tradition, we needed to let the project move in other directions.

At the same time, we decided to tie in our year-end open house with the art program and exhibit our students' work instead of taking it out on the streets in the parade. We changed the conceptual frame. Instead of bringing the students out into the community to show what their work looks like collectively, we are now creating collaborative projects within the school. In this way we are also focusing on school-site improvement, aesthetics, and making visible the power of collective energy. We permanently installed the mural of self-portraits in a school stairwell and we continue to create permanent and semipermanent installations from the work of all of our students in first through fifth grades.

The changes in Sequoia's arts program responded to our context. We focused on what we are moving toward, meaningful arts integration, not what we gave up. And we realize this process of change will continue.

STEP 4: PROFESSIONAL DEVELOPMENT
FOR SCHOOLWIDE ARTS INTEGRATION

In the fall of 2007, Sequoia was chosen to participate as one of Oakland's Arts Anchor Schools. With Anchor School funding, we are focusing on professional development for teachers in art and arts integration. We realized that teachers' knowledge, skill, and confidence are the lynchpins for making the most of arts integration. As a result, teachers are learning about and from the arts, reenvisioning their planning and teaching, creating arts-integrated curricula, and placing art at the center of their thinking about children and learning. For many teachers, this is a welcome change from the more rigidly scripted and monitored curriculum programs and professional development that have been imposed upon them. Now, an already existing arts program, created with the intention of connecting to classroom curricula, is being leveraged to move the school toward a holistic vision of incorporating art into the faculty's everyday teaching practices. The vision of the Art Is Education! initiative of Art for Every Child, in Every Classroom, Every Day has the potential to be realized at Sequoia because the art program is well established, the artist in residence has strong and long-standing relationships with the stable faculty, and the principal is strongly committed to arts integration.

A dynamic art program and a receptive faculty are still not enough to create schoolwide arts integration across the curriculum, however. While we had great examples of visual arts/language arts connections, and many instances where the art making truly helped inspire more complex writing on the part of students, we still had not made art a meaningful component of every child's every day in every classroom so that arts learning could be leveraged to help children understand material across the curriculum.

To reach this goal, Sequoia Elementary decided to focus specifically on integrating visual arts and language arts and is using the opportunity of the Arts Anchor initiative to hone the writing and verbal language skills of students at every grade level. At the same time, faculty is being coached by the Bay Area Writing Project, attempting to look at an array of issues that prevent students from excelling in writing.

Teachers are also learning about art. They have learned to use basic drawing, collage, watercolor, and printmaking in their classrooms. I meet monthly with teachers who have the opportunity to work with the same materials that are simultaneously being taught to their students. Teachers observe their students' art instruction, paying attention to their learning in art and other disciplines. Teachers participate as learners during the students' art instruction as well. In the process, teachers are finding their personal way of making visual art a part of their teaching habits, one step at a time. All the teachers, even a few self-proclaimed "art phobic" teachers, have participated in the visual art professional development and have gained confidence in their own artistic abilities. All the teachers at the very least use art in some new way in their classrooms. In professional development meetings, teachers share successes and brainstorm ideas to create meaningful connections between visual art and literacy. The meetings contribute to a strong, positive energy among the faculty, a sense of collaborative purpose, and fun.

Art classes have evolved to create stronger connections to literacy through visual arts. We received a donation of blank sketchbooks, which children used for drawing throughout the year. The journals have become a place where students can reflect in writing on their artwork and where they can return to see the visible progress they have made through the year as artists and writers. We set aside time for children to observe and reflect on their progress. The necessity for this might appear obvious, but allowing the opportunity for reflection was a big shift on my part. I had not spent very much time with reflections in the past, as I would get caught up in the whirlwind of activity and the limits of time when I was trying to work on messy, complicated, and extended projects. Now I see reflection helping students and teachers connect arts learning to writing.

Teachers are integrating art and connecting it to the curriculum across the curriculum. Two third-grade teachers used visual art to help children gain understanding of a difficult math concept. They asked students to draw imaginary creatures out of various kinds of polygons and then to describe their character in writing. Borrowing an idea from professional development, the same third-grade teachers asked students to observe works of art, describe what they saw, and write interpretations. One tech-savvy teacher put various photographic images on a Web site and then asked students to choose an image and respond to that image with a poem. A fourth-grade teacher, very involved in the Sequoia garden, frequently took her students out to the garden with their sketchbooks, where they documented with drawings and recorded in writing the plants' changes and growth. Fifth-grade teachers created "A Day in the Life of a Shoe," which asked students to make a careful observational drawing of one of their shoes and then write an account of its meanderings.

As we continue our work as an Arts Anchor school, we are trying to craft our professional development, our art program, and our meeting time to make arts integration an effective tool of learning, particularly in writing across the disciplines. We are focusing student learning on visual art and written and oral language and focusing the range of art materials and processes on drawing, watercolor, collage, printmaking, and book arts. Teachers feel they need more time to experiment with the arts now that they have begun to get familiar with them, in order to make the visual arts their own and to feel comfortable using art as a tool.

Learning and taking something on as part of one's own practice is a protracted and messy business, for seasoned teachers as much as for young children. At Sequoia we value teachers' arts learning as much as the students'. And consequently, as teachers reflect on their own arts learning, we see the possibility of promoting students' deep understanding across the curriculum. And to think, it all started with a puppet parade!

CHAPTER 7

Musical People, a Musical School

Sarah Willner

WHAT ROLE DOES music have in our school community? To consider this question, one must ask, where does music live within children, within each person in the community? As a music teacher, I'm a weaver of a web, bringing out the music that already exists in the students' heads, in the experiences and hands of their family and ancestors, and on the radio and Internet. I play with schoolyard jump-rope rhymes and the DJ mix shortcuts that the older students whiz through on the computer. I introduce music that my students do not yet know. I teach, discover, champion, and make music together with my students, their families, and our faculty and staff. What potential expression of musicality and movement is now in my students' heads and hands? To understand, let's take a tour of my school. After the tour I will describe some of the reasons why we should integrate music across the curriculum and how student learning benefits. I conclude with examples of music integration from my own school, where all teachers are committed to practicing the arts as an expression of learning and identity and a means of reflection.

A MUSICAL TOUR

Walk into ASCEND School first thing in the morning, past bright murals and intriguing artwork. ASCEND (A School Cultivating Equity, Nurturing Diversity) was opened in 2001, one of the first experiments of the small schools movement within the Oakland Unified School District. From the school's inception, arts learning has been one of the central tenets. I have had the good fortune to be one of the original teachers at this amazing model.

It's not even 8:00 a.m., yet the middle school band is pounding out "Caribbean Delight." They and their parents sacrifice their sleeping hours for the reward of playing an instrument. The bell rings for the actual school day start, and "This Land Is Your Land" and "Somos Paz" drift down to the open foyer: the primary grades sing together once a week in the library. Parents sit at the back of the room with younger siblings in baby carriages, augmenting their own English skills, proud that their children are carrying on songs their families sang in their home language and participating in the culture of American songs. In the "Primary Sing," kindergarten students might perform a song they wrote about the life cycle of a seed, part of an integrated unit on food production. With suggestions, the other teachers and I find and lead the eclectic songs: seasonal and celebratory, pop, peace and social justice, funny and silly, for the ancestors, and about the cycle of life. Each primary class starts each day of the week with its own or these same songs.

Continuing the tour outward to community: Perhaps the special day class for children with mental or emotional disorders and hearing disabilities is heading out the door on their way to perform songs and original poems with instrumental accompaniment at the preschool down the street. These preschoolers are our next year's kindergarteners; they now know that songs are important in their future school. The seventh grade may also be leaving for the senior center down the block, armed with songs from their own parents' heritage to share with the seniors as a community service component of a history project, "Honoring Elders." These students connect to their audience, as the seniors sing and dance along, and then pay them back with treasured songs of their own.

Lunchtime: Eighth-grade girls rush in to practice their graduation song or speech for me. Others borrow a CD player to practice an original dance for an after-school talent show. Students gather for tips on applying to and auditioning for city and local summer programs in dance, fine arts, and music. A very few eighth graders apply for an arts magnet high school, while others wonder if they will ever make music or art again. The hope is that the arts become one of the languages in which ASCEND students are fluent. Our ethic is that the arts are for everyone; they are part of our world, rather than just for the "talented" few. In addition to regular classes, consider the following activities:

Recess and PE: Jump-rope and clapping games. Students are drumming on the swing set and quoting a rap about tennis shoes while shooting their baskets. The teachers eat lunch, iPods playing jazz, metal, and Cuban hip-hop, or perhaps a civil rights song that they will need in tomorrow's history lesson.

Optional after-school: The African drum teacher hauls in his gorgeous percussion battery, the hip-hop dance teachers plug in the boombox, the choir teacher stomps her time-keeping staff. The students enter into specific art forms here, two or three times a week. This specialization builds musical skills and weds the student to their art form, over and above the general music enrichment classes and the arts integration. The after-school classes are bridges to a wide variety of artistic communities.

Visiting guests and parent artists: Rom musicians tune up bouzoukis and ouds, their nomadic history intriguing to these children of immigrants; an Azteca *danzante* lays out his masks and tortoiseshell percussion, reminding these largely Mexican American students of their pre-Columbian roots; a gospel singer hands out charts of slavery-era code songs. A Mien parent carefully slips an old cassette out of her intricately embroidered purse. On it is the only extant recording of an a capella ballad her family commissioned to memorialize her father, killed in the 1970s secret wars in Laos. Guest artists, including parents, are an invaluable part of the fabric of arts-integrated projects in the classroom during the regular school day. They also coach cultural dances and mentor students in the arts during recess and after school.

Upstairs to the Family Center, which, in conjunction with the after-school program, leads various cultural events throughout the year: These programs have sometimes highlighted a single ethnic group at the school, such as Mien, African American, or Mexican American. Sometimes their focus is pan-cultural; in 2007, Tongan dance took the stage along with a Mien flower dance, a waltzing Filipino candle dance, Los Viejitos from Mexico, Brazilian samba, and Vietnamese pop. Students decorated the stage with African masks and world flags. Music is a readily recognized way to connect to culture.

Even the custodians and lunch coordinator are valued mentors, singing solos with the choir and coaching cheerleading, Tongan dance, and drum line. The artistic momentum is self-perpetuating in this community.

WHY A MUSICAL SCHOOL?

What is significant about a "musical school"? Why shouldn't music just stay in the music class, taught by an expert? On the other hand, why have music classes at all? One might argue that there is no worldwide decline in listening, sharing, or buying music. Making music on computer programs like GarageBand has never been easier. And why integrate music into other subjects, when already there is practically no time for any subject not on the test? Does integration dilute music making?

My inquiry into the musicality of my students both in and out of music class is inspired by Campbell (1998), who researched where and how children interact with music: in line going down the hall, sitting in the lunchroom, in their minds while writing a test, on the school bus, as well as in the music class, at church, and at home. She writes, "In important ways, the home and school—and the efforts of parents and teachers—can take children from who they musically are to all that they can musically become" (p. 223).

As a music teacher, I feel that I must also research, acknowledge, and in various ways encourage all the music my students experience and express. We build on their varied musical experiences by bringing them into the music classroom and onstage. At the same time, it is my job to introduce forms of music and music making that are not in my students' or their families' experiences, as a component of an equitable education. It is by making and bringing together the music from in and out of class, from in and out of minds, from in and out of families, that we create and enact a culture together at this school in the heart of such a culturally diverse city.

Take a musical tour of your own day. What role does music play in your journey to or from school? Are you relating rhythmically to other people as you adjust your movement down the sidewalk? Walking outside, does a note sound just under your breath as you observe the weather? Take a musical tour of your school. Listen and observe musicality in your community. Students hum melodies to themselves and their desk partner as they write; their shake-shake-shake-up of lunchtime milk is an allied engine of hips, elbows, and shoulders. Inches outside the school doors at the end of day, earphones snake upward out of pockets as middle school students define identity with their own music choices.

WHY LEARN THROUGH MUSIC?

Sachs (2007) affirms that "we humans are a musical species no less than a linguistic one. . . . Our auditory systems, our nervous systems, are indeed exquisitely tuned for music" (p. xi). Our brains are wired for music as thoroughly as they have evolved for language. And yet Goodkin (2006) notes, "The amount of music instruction that the average American school child receives in one year is equal to the amount of time she or he spends watching TV in one week." Why neglect this deeply rooted human intelligence and treasure? The answer is to bring music into the center of the curriculum. While music making itself must be paramount, music and music integration can be a springboard into learning and thinking in other disciplines.

As an arts integration coach at the school, Lois Hetland reminded faculty, "In integration, each of the two subjects to be integrated must be authentically present." To integrate music and other subject areas effectively, we must deeply enter into the world of music as well as the other discipline with which it is integrated. Students develop understanding from the "metacognitive hugging" that goes on when two disciplines embrace and explore each other. For the arts to be meaningfully integrated and not just serving other academic work (e.g., singing the alphabet song), students need also to be thinking and questioning explicitly in the arts as well as in other disciplines.

The studio habits of mind (Hetland, Winner, Veenema, & Sheridan, 2007) were developed by looking at the thinking required for and developed by making visual art. Although I reference these habits, more useful to this chapter is a framework that Gardiner (2000, p. 72) developed specifically about music learning. He describes five different ways that music can have value to education:

- Values specific to music: Creation and performance of music
- Music instruction as a support for other topics of learning: music as it mirrors history and culture; music as it makes audible patterns, forms, and relationships

- Effects of music on attitudes and mental skills broadly useful to learning: learning self-reflection; practice and perseverance
- Effects of music instruction on specific subcomponents of mental skills useful to subcomponents of learning
- Music as an aid to social/emotional and personal development: for example, working in an ensemble, playing as a soloist or as a soloist within an ensemble, and communicating with an audience.

On our tour we saw examples of music illustrating every one of Gardiner's points, with the two major sites for music education within the school day being enrichment and arts integration classes. You can also see how Gardiner's framework and the studio habits of mind share some important similarities, which I will describe in the following paragraphs.

In the enrichment classes at ASCEND, the arts teachers emphasize arts skills that support larger projects and ideas across a variety of subject areas. For example, perhaps the fifth graders are studying immigration. During music time we may polish the conga technique for a Caribbean song bringing together African, Spanish, and indigenous elements. This is where Gardiner's first point lives: values specific to music (similar to the studio habits of developing craft and expressing). In many schools the arts stop with the comparative luxury and possible isolation of enrichment classes in music or a band class that focuses on skills. But arts learning throughout the curriculum is an especially valuable way to access and express learning, as well as engage in metacognition.

ASCEND stands out from most schools integrating the arts because of the quantity and quality of arts integration, supporting Gardiner's second point about the value of music education, "Music instruction as a support for other topics of learning: music as it mirrors history and culture; music as it makes audible patterns and forms relationships."

We can connect this value to the studio habit of "understanding the art world." We can also see the arts in context, our studio habit now reframed into "understanding arts in the world." We will explore this value in the examples of arts integration that follow later in the chapter.

Gardiner's third and fourth values of music in education, "Effects of music on attitudes and mental skills broadly useful to learning" and "effects on specific subcomponents" speak to the studio habits like reflecting, engaging and persisting, envisioning, observing, and stretching and exploring.

Gardiner's fifth musical value, "Music as an aid to social/emotional and personal development," describes how music strengthens both individual endeavor and an awareness of the good of the group. Musicians must mindfully balance themselves on this axis.

Interestingly, the studio habits of mind overlap and support the central moral tenets of behavior and relationship at the heart of the school, called the "Six Ways to ASCEND." For example, reflection on one's work, behavior, and process is a constant in every class at ASCEND. If two students are in a fight, the first thing they are asked to do is write a reflection about the incident. Similarly, in the arts, when musicians sing and artists exhibit at the school, they post statements and programs reflecting on their work. Photos, videos, and drafts show the journey they took to the gallery and the stage.

ARTS INTEGRATION IN THE MUSICAL SCHOOL

As part of the core curriculum alongside language arts and math, each ASCEND grade works on two "expeditions" (Cousins, 2000) a year. Similar to project-based learning and thematic teaching units, ASCEND's expeditions often start with a standards-based social studies or science focus. The expeditions follow a line of inquiry with guiding questions and include a strong writing component, opportunity for community engagement, and, of course, visual art and music (and even possibly other arts) as part of the learning and expression of learning.

In the ASCEND model, the classroom teachers and the arts teachers work together in the same room, 1 hour a week with music, 1 hour a week with visual arts, for one semester. Crucial to using the artists' time efficiently is the grade-level collaboration of classroom teachers. Sometimes the teachers in a grade will specialize and take on only one of the arts, over the years gaining a fluency and comfort with that art form. Classroom teachers spend the second semester on expeditions where they are the primary guide of the arts, with some resources and planning support from the arts teachers. The expeditions repeat from year to year, so that the teachers can refine their units as well as their arts-teaching skills.

You might be slightly mystified about why the students work with two art forms, art and music, during a single expedition. Wouldn't it be better to work with visual art in this botany expedition and in music for the Harlem Renaissance? Yet, second /third-grade teacher Hatti Saunders reminds us that "in any one area, there may be students that only 'get it' through a certain modality. Which is why you need more than one art form relating to a subject. There may be a student who really gets the life cycle of a seed by acting it out, while another student really benefits from the time spent in observational drawing of the seed, sprout, and stem." Further, working on one expedition through both art forms necessarily supports collaboration and professional development. In the majority of teaching situations, arts teachers work alone. By collaborating, arts teachers have allies in the classroom teachers and in each other. The goal of arts integration is not to obviate the need for an arts teacher. Rather, the better the classroom teachers understand an art through hands-on experience and practice, the better they can work by themselves to integrate it into their curriculum and also the better they can work with an arts specialist.

EXAMPLES OF ARTS INTEGRATION IN THE MUSICAL SCHOOL

These stories about arts integration and arts learning from Grades K, 1, 2, 3, and 7 are meant to provide inspiration for how to integrate music with a variety of discipline areas. They illustrate the "metacognitive hugging" when students go deep into more than one discipline. The examples also illustrate how music teachers and general classroom teachers can work together and learn from one another.

Kindergarten

ASCEND's kindergarten teacher Alexandra Kulka provides two examples of how music and writing/reading leverage learning across these two areas of the curriculum. Alexandra first suggested that we connect music class to the students' journal writing. The students were literally jazzed up after music class and inspired to write and draw about what they had just done. After the active music making—singing, moving, beat keeping, instrument playing in ensemble and solo—students discussed prompts that Alexandra and I had come up with, for example, What was your favorite part of music class? How do you play a xylophone? Was anything difficult, and how did you work on it? What might be the next scene in our play? After modeling some responses to the prompt as a class, each student wrote and drew in her or his journal. In struggling to communicate in writing and drawing about their musical experience, the students, mostly English learners, leveraged music time toward better literacy skills and vocabulary.

I could not have had the insight into how to teach writing. As they wrote and drew in their journals, I would stay in the room, roving to support their individual writing. I was the special music teacher and not their classroom teacher, and they were thrilled to show me exactly how they had depicted their experience. I could also help supply specific vocabulary and reminders about what we had done. Ms. Kulka and I were assisting each other in our primary area of expertise and learning how to teach and support the other curricular area. We became aware of what the other teacher was looking for in students' writing and music.

Alexander Pope asks, "What will a child learn sooner than a song?" Brain research shows that there is not a single music center in the brain. Involvement in music affects so many parts of the brain: Different areas join for hearing and remembering, more areas are called into play for understanding lyrics, others to coordinate physical playing, and more again for experiencing the emotions music creates; putting it all together to make meaning with music lights up the brain like a burning bush.

The next example of minds alight, from Ms. Kulka's class, illustrates how music instruction supports the skills and dispositions useful to learning, particularly reading. All year the students sang, mainly learning material through aural/oral transmission, supported by charts. Toward the end of the year we examined our extensive collection of songbooks in the classroom, then gathered up all the songs the students knew into our own class songbook. Each student put the pages together into a book and illustrated their songs, often drawing upon their journaling.

We sat down and opened the songbook. I asked, "Please put your finger on the first word and follow along as we sing the song." The students sang the words they knew with gusto. They already had many of the lyrics memorized and were starting to know beginning sounds of words written on the page: The two came together in the songbook. Almost all the little index fingers were traveling in diligent concert across the page, even returning to the top of the page for the chorus. Ms. Kulka and I almost jumped up and down. "They're reading! They're reading!" The students' worlds came together. Before knowing those words in the context of the song, they most likely could not have read them. Now that they knew them— even mastered them in the singing—they would have a much better chance at being able to read them again in other contexts.

First Grade

One especially successful expedition was a first-grade "family project," with classroom teachers Kathryn Fireman and Linda Sciera. When we pick a subject, we try to make it as rich as possible in opportunities for music making, in specific studio habits of mind, and in social considerations. We wanted the process of learning about family to help strengthen the students' home families and "school family."

We knew that this class had extraordinarily avid singers, able at such a young age to sing in four-part rounds and two-part harmony. The classroom teachers suggested making a CD and songbook of family songs, which could be sold to raise money for performing arts field trips. As we sent notes home with our mini-musicologists asking for "family" songs, I realized my stereotyping presumptuousness in expecting families to maintain a storehouse of songs from an oral tradition. After all, how many Lithuanian milking songs do I, the descendant of such immigrants, hum around the house? The African American child may never have heard a spiritual; the Mexican American child's home music may very likely consist solely of Disney hits, and hip-hop is often the most meaningful genre for a Mien family. As it turned out, the music that most connected students to their generational roots were lullabies, such as "Duermate Mi Niño."

We recorded many different categories of pieces around the theme of family. We added new lyrics and percussion to Abby Lincoln's "I Got Some People In Me." In addition, the classroom teachers guided the students to write their own song about the empathy and caring that it takes to get along in our home families and in our family at school. Three of the CD's tracks are a collage of interviews with the students and teachers about what a family does (takes care of each other, has fun with each other, etc.), as well as possible reasons why different families sing different versions of the same lullaby.

What better way to reach out to our community than including the families actually singing on the CD? At a meeting of all the first-grade families, we recorded parents singing our bilingually adapted version of John McCutcheon's "Is My Family." The lyrics begin in the small arena of family with the verse "This tiny house with the roof above" and move outward to the larger community of "*la escuelita donde mi hijo va* [the school my child attends]" and finally to "this great big world all the way around." The parents also performed this song with their children at the CD-release party to a teary-eyed audience. Some parents and grandparents formed duets with their child, passing on in this recording project songs they learned from their own parents. In performing these songs live at the biannual Exposition of Learning and on the CD, we gave them to our other "family," our school community, which we helped create through the singing.

Second Grade

How does an integrated curriculum serve the students? According to second-grade teacher Hatti Saunders, "With musical experiences and with music integration, more hooks are created in their minds from which to make more connections." Her second graders wrote their own story, "Cinderella in Hawaii," after reading different versions of the tale from around the world and deconstructing them for common story elements. One pair of students created an antagonist after brainstorming characteristics: greedy, cold, mean, and so on. What descriptive detail might be gained in also drawing the character? What else might we learn about how the character thinks and acts if we create a musical theme and a soundtrack for various episodes in the character's life, or even write songs that that character sings? We could practically hear the firing of synapses as the children translated between modes of expression, and between the vocabularies of the different disciplines. Second grader Teresa Cole, a principle "Cinderella" composer, exclaimed, "It's so easy to write the words when I can sing them!" Working within developmentally appropriate musical scales, bolstered by her knowledge of her island protagonist's situation, Teresa wrote melody and lyrics for Cinderella's lament, and Jabari Jones accompanied it with a drip-drop pattern in Ionian mode on the silvery glockenspiel. April Saechao sang out, "Every coconut I pick, I drop a little tear."

Third Grade

In a previous year, the third-grade focus was on autobiography's interplay with a famous Oakland musical genre, the blues. Instead of learning many songs, one rich piece was chosen as the center of the expedition. What comes before the piece that informs it? African American musical history. How can we play the piece rigorously with all the skills needed? Musical scales, improvising over chord changes, and a 12-bar form. How can we communicate through a musical genre? The creation of our own blues. What is going on socially within the school that can be helped by the study of this form? The Latino and African American students' understanding of their own and each other's culture and history.

A study of the 12-bar blues served all the musical skills and understandings exactly at our students' level, hitting a large number of the state grade-level music standards along the way. The students each wrote and sang a verse of "The Fruitvale Blues" to celebrate the vibrant neighborhood where most of them live. They accompanied themselves on the Orff xylophone orchestra, which is a handy tool for making the blues scales visible. The music did not exactly connect to our majority Latino culture, but we used the blues form to tell the story of Fruitvale and introduce our students to a new cultural expression for which parts of their city are famous.

In the blues project, we started by viewing videos and listening to blues artists from the early decades of the 20th century. How was blues related to Africa, spirituals, rock, and hip-hop? Oakland was a blues beehive in the 1970s and 1980s, and Ishmael Reed, a famous local author, wrote a book about Oakland, *Blues City* (2003). We decided to view our own neighborhood, the Fruitvale, through blues eyes.

Guest artists from the non-profit Oakland Blues Caravan played guitar and drum for and with us. Ultimately, they invited our students to open one of their centerpiece events: the West Coast Blues and Gospel Awards Gala. Blinded by the sequins, intrigued by the smoke coming out of the next dressing room, forty students in their ASCEND uniforms braved the glare of the lights and sang and played "Fruitvale Blues," written by two students, to the roaring crowd.

> *Pigeons only sit on telephone lines*
> *Pigeons only sit on telephone lines*
> *There isn't much nature in the Fruitvale.*

> *I've got a car called a low-rider*
> *I've got a car called a low-rider*
> *We ride in Fruitvale, International Boulevard.*

> *My mom came to Fruitvale in a coyote's truck*
> *My mom came to Fruitvale in a coyote's truck*
> *She made it to Oakland. La Migra didn't catch her.*

Seventh Grade

What happens when musicians and music teachers are not in the classroom? ASCEND teachers are expected to continue to integrate the arts on their own, with the musicians and artists acting as resources. Middle school humanities teacher Katherine Suyeyasu's experience illustrates how being a music learner leads to becoming a music teacher.

Katherine wanted to teach a Jewish song and dance to her students as part of a comparative study of religions, a piece that would convey core Jewish beliefs, preferably with a wonderful melody. She needed a song of an appropriate difficulty in terms of language for her group of mainly English language learners, with a pitch suitable for middle school changing voices. These seventh graders had come to our school only the year before, without any prior musical training, so Katherine also needed hands-on training tips on how to warm up her students' voices, convey starting pitch and tempo, and get middle school students to sing in tune. She undertook the song and dance "Ma Navu" after assisting me with the Christian spirituals portion of the comparative religion project. She started by leading small groups of students in song, with percussion or xylophone accompaniment. Then she practiced leading the whole class of 24 students, again, after observation. She led the class in performance of the piece, which her students then taught to another class. After continued reflection with her class Katherine is in a powerful position to lead discussion of how the song helps teach about Jewish beliefs, history, and social interaction. She also knows how to work with a music specialist and is much more confident about leading music making.

Most important, these students gained metacognitive understanding. Interviewed in 2006 for an educational television profile of arts integration at ASCEND School, seventh grader Crystal Garcia said, "We get to experience learning in a different way, not just reading out of a text." Her classmate Mary White agreed, "If it's just out of a textbook, they'd say, 'Do you understand?' And I'd say no, because I can't really visualize it. But if you're actually doing it, I can actually understand it."

MUSIC AT THE CENTER

Elena Aguilar, one of the original ASCEND middle school teachers, follows graduates through high school and college. From interviews with them, she has found that it is often dispositions like those in the studio habits of mind that have helped students. "At ASCEND we were always told to persevere. I would not still be in school if I didn't," reported one student. Another said, "Reflection has helped me get through high school. We were so sick of that word at ASCEND! But I learned how to think about my situation, take charge of my own life."

ASCEND students and graduates are the house musicians, poets, rappers, and organizers of the All-Oakland Talent Show. One of my former students has made a film about how dancing has saved his life. These young people make peace murals, exhibit portraits at city hall, and design their local library logo. ASCEND graduates teach and coach arts, academics, and life skills in high school internships and paid jobs; some now have started college. Their parents continue to fight to preserve this schooling for their community, armed with their children's words, art, and songs.

San Francisco music teacher and philosopher Doug Goodkin asks us to conceive of a different paradigm. "Instead of the stiffness of 'Watch carefully! Now entering an arts-integrated zone!' why not position music at the center of the curriculum and the school community?"* The example of ASCEND illustrates the depth and richness of student learning when music is at the center of a school.

ACKNOWLEDGMENTS

Sincere thanks to all ASCEND students and their families, as well as all my colleagues and loved ones: Jen Stuart and David Donahue, Arzu Mistry, Louise Music, Arlene Schmaeff, Brett Wilson, Hatti Saunders, Kathryn Fireman, Larissa Adam, Natasha Zolp-McCray, Roxanne Padgett, Katherine Suyeyasu, Lois Hetland, Lisa Ostapinski, Doug Goodkin, Alexandra Kulka, Hae-sin Kim, Miranda Bergman, Angela Wellman, and Wayne Vitale.

REFERENCES

Campbell, P. S. (1998). *Songs in their heads: Music and its meaning in children's lives.* New York: Oxford University Press.

Cousins, E. (2000). *Roots: From Outward Bound to expeditionary learning.* Dubuque, IA: Kendell Hunt.

Gardiner, M. F. (2000). Music learning and behavior: A case for mental stretching. *Journal for Learning Through Music, 1,* 72–93.

Goodkin, D. (2006). *ABC's of education.* San Francisco: Pentatonic Press.

Hetland, L., Winner, E., Veenema, S., & Sheridan, K. (2007). *Studio thinking: The real benefits of visual arts education.* New York: Teachers College Press.

Reed, I. (2003). *Blues city: A walk in Oakland.* New York: Crown.

Sachs, O. (2007). *Musicophilia.* New York: Alfred A. Knopf.

---

*The comment was made in February 2005 at a workshop sponsored by the Alameda County Office of Education on classroom and music teaching.

PART IV

Art Every Day

CHAPTER 8

Visual Prompts
in Writing Instruction

Working with Middle School
English Language Learners

Dafney Blanca Dabach

I HAD BEEN HIRED to teach a writing class for English learners at a small public middle school in a bustling urban neighborhood in San Francisco. My principal wanted to make sure that English learners were being served, despite their small numbers in our school, and enlisted me in his efforts to make a difference.

Because I grew up in a multilingual immigrant home, I understood that my immigrant students brought rich language skills with them. But I also knew from my own family's experience that if my students did not fully develop their academic writing in English, their future opportunities would be limited. I felt an especially keen sense of pressure—what was I going to do that would make a difference? In my search I did what many teachers do: I dug deep within myself to search for possibilities. I turned to my background in photography to think about what connections I could make between the written word and the image and how looking at (or making) visual images could develop and promote writing. To me this seemed a natural connection; growing up I gravitated to photography as another form of expression. If my home life was mediated by the constant code-switching in and out of various spoken languages, photography became yet another form of language—a visual language where I could create, translate, and communicate ideas and emotions across cultural boundaries. It made sense that I would turn to one form of expression to help my students develop another: academic writing in English.

While there were many ways that I experimented with integrating visual art in my teaching practice that year, here I focus on one in particular: using image prompts for writing. I focus on this particular way of integrating the arts because it is one of the most accessible starting points, because it can easily be done every day, and because of what it revealed to me about my students as well as the writing instruction process.

WRITING FROM VISUAL PROMPTS
AS A SPACE FOR EXPERIMENTATION

Every day my students came into my classroom to find a writing "warm-up" exercise waiting for them. In this way I was able to maximize my students' learning time—as soon as they walked into the classroom, they knew that they were supposed to be engaged in writing.

This warm-up time at the beginning of class was also a space for both my students and me to experiment: I could experiment with assigning different types of visual prompts and my students could experiment with their writing, suspending—at least temporarily—the pressure to produce perfect or "correct" written language and actually practice the art of writing freely. In this sense, the key studio habit of mind (Hetland, Winner, Veenema, & Sheridan, 2007) that I was targeting was *expression*. By using visual prompts, I was also targeting two other studio habits: students' *observation* as well as their ability to *envision* beyond the frame to produce a narrative.

Over the course of the year, I began to notice that certain pictures would evoke particular responses—much like a Rorschach ink blot test. Sometimes my students' responses revealed their inner life, particular to themselves as individuals. Other times, when the same photograph evoked a similar response across a number of students, I would sense that I stumbled onto some aspect of collective experience—something beyond the individual student, and part of something larger. For example, I was drawn to one image, in particular, which evoked strong narrative possibilities. I selected it as a prompt because I wanted my students to think about generating and structuring stories.

Take a moment to look at the photograph by Micha Bar-Am, *The Return from Entebbe* (1998). What stories reside within this photograph? Imagine that this image presents a scene from a story you are writing (either fiction or nonfiction). Would this scene occur at the beginning, middle, or end of your story? Where does it fit within the narrative you imagine? If you are willing to experiment, before reading on, try writing from this image prompt.

LEARNING ABOUT STUDENTS' STORIES

How did students respond? Most students wrote war stories, with the above scene as the beginning journey of a son leaving to join the army in Iraq, or returning after a near-death experience while in the army in Iraq. The photo actually documents

Figure 8.1. *The Return from Entebbe.*

© Micha Bar-Am/Magnum Photos.

a reunion of a related but different sort. Photojournalist Micha Bar-Am took it in the aftermath of an airplane hostage rescue in 1976.

While students projected their own knowledge, fears, and sentiments to animate their stories, they could observe the emotional tenor of the photograph—the tight embraces; the physical closeness; the multiple people closely embracing one formerly, or soon to be, absent person; the multiple sets of hands that all reach out to touch one person; the mixed expressions of grief and relief on the faces of the women who are pictured. All these elements combined and informed their stories that communicated separation, danger, and reunion—all reinterpreted into the current political conflict in Iraq. They noticed and observed particular details specific to the photograph and blended this with their own perspectives and imaginations. This suggests that part of the value of visual prompts is how they reveal student thinking and perspectives, sometimes of a shared political or historical moment and other times of a situation more specific to themselves or their families. For example, while most of the students wrote about Iraq, one student who had recently come from Mexico wrote a story of a young man about to leave his family in Mexico to go to El Norte. This, too, reveals his experience and that of many migrants. When faced with a particular visual prompt, such as the Bar-Am photo, students can write stories that reveal their inner worlds, perspectives, and experiences.

As I started presenting visual prompts more regularly, I began to think more deeply about the types of responses that they would generate. Wanting to introduce social justice themes in my prompts, I was inspired to share photographer Sebastião Salgado's photographs (1993, 1997, 2000a, 2000b) with my class. His approach of documenting social inequality, poverty, and migration allowed me to raise such issues in my classroom with visual writing prompts. Salgado's massive photographic works on poverty, workers, migrants, and children have created a powerful and large opus documenting social inequalities worldwide. His work belongs to the social realism school (also present in the works of U.S. photographers like Dorothea Lange, who documented the human face of poverty during the Depression). Originally an economist, highly literate in the language of mathematics, Salgado took to the camera in desperation because he found that his economic reports could not possibly convey the gravity of poverty in his native Brazil.

Take a look at the photo by Salgado, *Kurdistan—Little Girl* (2000a, p. 15). To begin with, what would you imagine the child's name is? How would you describe her daily life? In examining my students' responses to this image, I was struck by three responses in particular:

> *Minh, seventh grade, from Vietnam, length of residence 2 years:* "Her life it [is] not fair."
> *Marcelo, sixth grade, from Mexico, length of residence 2 years:* "She like[s] to play soccer."
> *Ernesto, seventh grade, from Mexico, length of residence 3 years:* "Nina is so skinny because she doesn't have no money to buy food. She is freezing because she lives in Alaska. Her eyes are very dark green that she looks like a monster. Her stomach growls like dog. She is so pale that you could see her veins."

Figure 8.2. *Kurdistan—Little Girl.*

© Sebastião Salgado/Amazonas Images/Contact Press Images.

These three students demonstrate very different responses to the same photograph. While Minh's response reveals limited written production, even his five-word response captures the social justice message embedded in the photograph; Minh is able to express, at the most basic level, the unfairness of the child's existence. Marcelo, on the other hand, writes about how the young refugee, pictured wearing sandals in the snow, likes to play soccer—something which bears no trace of a suggestion in the photograph. However, knowing that Marcelo's great passion in life is soccer, I concluded that this exercise revealed much more about Marcelo than about the girl in the photograph. His interpretation of the girl in the photograph had become a mirror image of himself. Since *he* likes to play soccer, so does *she*. As a teacher, this gives me clues to pursue in understanding Marcelo and his interests, as well as ideas for specialized prompts that are based on his interests. Finally, Ernesto's response reveals how the photograph provokes his own imagination and language production, with imaginative metaphoric details inspired by evidence in the photograph. Taken together, these three students' writing reveals how the visual prompt adds an important tool for writing instruction that produces different and valuable responses from students.

In thinking about students' responses overall, I have noticed that students vary in the degree to which they attend to details of a particular image. Some are highly attentive to looking closely, while others quickly get a flash of inspiration for a story and begin writing immediately, sometimes barely looking at the image prompt. Either way, their responses still reveal a great deal about their own perspectives. When thinking about my role in fostering students' observation, I think back to the day when Ernesto, Marcelo, and Minh were writing their responses. While Ernesto in particular seems to have observed closely and used his observations to inspire his imagination, I also remember being by his side, asking him questions about the image and what he noticed. I also remember that time ran out before I was able to talk with Marcelo about his work. Thinking back on my own role, I wish I could have asked Marcelo more questions about what he was noticing in the photograph and helped direct his attention on a deeper level. Or perhaps in conversation I would have learned that he was missing vocabulary to express what he was noticing. Looking together at a shared visual artifact, I might have been able to better assist his vocabulary growth. Even so, I still learned more about Marcelo and his love of soccer through this process. I also considered the implications for whole-class instruction: modeling how to observe a photograph; notice details and ask questions; and finally, build a story from those details and questions.

QUESTIONS FOR THINKING ABOUT VISUAL WRITING PROMPTS

At this point you may be wondering about how to integrate visual prompts in your classroom. Rather than offering recipes, I offer a few questions to generate ideas:

1. *What kind of writing do I want my students to generate? (Or, Why am I picking particular images?)* You will want to choose an image that suits the kind of writing you hope students will produce. For example, at one point I wanted my students to practice writing with very simple sentences (because they were relying too heavily on long, convoluted sentences). I specifically chose a picture of a baby and asked them to write from the baby's perspective in simple sentences. In addition to considering the genre in which you want your students to write, you may also want to think about how the content in the image can prompt specific types of conversations—for example, social justice issues like war, poverty, and so on. How will the image I pick reflect particular themes or issues I would like to raise with my students? In thinking about this question I try to envision, What types of responses do I think the prompts will generate?

2. *What types of sources am I including or excluding when searching for images? What implications does this have?* For better or for worse, our society has an abundance of images in newspapers, books, magazines, and the Internet that are created and distributed for different purposes. Visual stereotypes can present an opportunity for critical reflection, but having an awareness of representation issues is important before introducing images to your class. How would you address problematic representation issues? How would you find alternative sources? One colleague of mine, Della Peretti, encourages student teachers to seek out magazines from barbershops and hair salons in the communities where their students live for a wider variety of images. Also, alternative history books (e.g., Martínez, 1990) present images often overlooked by traditional texts and other sources. My images come largely from photographs, but paintings and other visual art can provide excellent prompts as well.

3. *What kind of textual or verbal prompt will I use with the image?* Images do not necessarily speak for themselves. A few framing words in a clear written prompt can make a big difference. Instead of "write about what you see," try, "This picture is from a scene in a mystery novel you are writing. Begin writing the ending of this story." Think about why you selected a particular image, what you want students to accomplish in their writing, and what types of written framing devices in your prompt will help students achieve this. Specific writing instructions can potentially support creativity if the language helps students access a clear vision of possibilities.

4. *How am I going to support my students while they are writing?* Engage with students while they are looking at the prompts and even during or after their writing. A picture can be mined by students, especially when a teacher is close by to ask them questions about their interpretations—to push their thinking, observations, and hence what is available for their writing. The more you push students to notice details, the more they have available to write from. Asking them questions about what they see is a good approach

because it can encourage them to look deeper while still retaining their own interpretations. This is a practice you can model for the whole class.

Additional forms of support specifically for English language learner (ELL) students would include expanding vocabulary needed for expression, evaluating the language demands of the task, and scaffolding students' understanding of the prompt (Walqui, 2006). Walqui offers an in-depth understanding of the sociocultural concept of scaffolding and how it relates to ELL students. (She defines *scaffolding* as being part of the structural progression of lessons as well as the interactive means of assistance.) Rather than simplifying prompts, the use of scaffolding strategies such as contextualization, modeling, bridging, and schema building can enable students to do more than they would be able to do independently and have access to more complex language embedded in writing prompts.

CONCLUSION

As I searched for tools to improve my writing instruction, I realized that using images could provide my students with far richer prompts than text alone because of how powerfully the visual form connects to the written form. I also discovered that I had to carefully choose what types of pictures I would present to my students. My motto in choosing photographs for writing prompts became "Suit the picture to the task." For example, if I were interested in working on sentence structure, I would choose a photograph suggesting certain kinds of sentences. If plot and character development were what I was focusing on, then I would choose a different type of photo likely to evoke rich narratives. With planning and in-the-moment attentiveness, using visual prompts with purpose and depth is possible, even in the space of a classroom warm-up.

While I developed insights on how to integrate visual prompts into my writing instruction, I also noticed how my students' responses revealed their thoughts, perspectives, and experiences. Sometimes their responses revealed collective experiences, while other times their responses revealed more about what was on a particular student's mind.

Drawing from an equity-based pedagogy that stresses understanding students' strengths and not simply focusing on deficits means that using students' visual resources, in addition to other resources, is critical. Sight is an accessible resource that most students and teachers can draw upon, unless they are visually impaired. Typically, eyesight constitutes "our main source of information about the world, sending more data more quickly to the nervous system than any other sense" (Barry, 1997, p. 15). With so much information coming to us through our eyes, as conscientious educators how can we ignore visual media in teaching? While nearly all students can benefit from integrating visual images into writing instruction, for language learners, images provide an important opportunity to look closely—to concretely point, compare and observe, describe, imagine, and then write.

ACKNOWLEDGMENTS

I gratefully acknowledge helpful feedback from David Donahue, Julia Menard-Warwick, Chris Faltis, Rose Vilchez, and Joshua Meidav. I would also like to thank Paul Ammon, Patty Yancey, Ann Wettrich, and Jennifer Stuart for support in developing an arts-integrative practice. Finally, I would like to thank my students for being my teachers.

REFERENCES

Bar-Am, M. (1998). *Israel: A photobiography; The first 50 years.* New York: Simon & Schuster.

Barry, A. M. S. (1997). *Visual intelligence: Perception, image, and manipulation in visual communication.* Albany: SUNY Press.

Hetland, L., Winner, E., Veenema, S., & Sheridan, K. (2007). *Studio thinking: The real benefits of arts education.* New York: Teachers College Press.

Martínez, E. (1990). *500 años del pueblo chicano: 500 years of Chicano history.* Albuquerque, NM: Southwest Organizing Project.

Salgado, S. (1993). *Workers: An archaeology of the industrial age.* New York: Aperture.

Salgado, S. (1997). *Terra: Struggle of the landless.* London: Phaidon.

Salgado, S. (2000a). *The children: Refugees and migrants.* New York: Aperture.

Salgado, S. (2000b). *Migrations: Humanity in transition.* New York: Aperture.

Walqui, A. (2006). Scaffolding instruction for English language learners: A conceptual framework. *The International Journal of Bilingual Education and Bilingualism, 9*(2), 159–180.

CHAPTER 9

Creativity as Classroom Management

Using Drama and Hip-Hop

Evan Hastings

"PUT YOUR HEAD in the toilet!" said a student, playing the role of a bully in an improvisation. He stood firm and looked down at the student seated below him. The student in the seat shrunk and looked at the floor.

"I said put your head in the toilet or I'll put it there for you." Squirming in his seat, the student being bullied looked at me and I knew that this was too real for him right now.

I looked to the students who were currently playing the role of the audience and I asked, "What would you do in this situation? Raise your hand and I'll call on you." I invited the student who was playing the bullied character to step out of role and witness the other students' attempts at dealing with this bullying situation.

One student intervened by saying, "No! *You* put *your* head in the toilet," to the bully character. The underdogs in the class smiled. I asked the class, "Was this an effective and responsible way of dealing with the bully?" Some students thought it was responsible and effective, while others argued that provoking a bully is not a good idea.

I invited the students to try more alternative actions. One student sat in the chair of the bullied character and said, "No, I'm leaving." He stood up and walked away without looking back, then said, "I'm going to tell a teacher."

"What did you see him try? Was it responsible?" I asked. My question spurred a discussion about "snitching," or reporting someone else's behavior to any form of authority. Some students expressed a view that snitching is irresponsible because it invites retaliation, while other students thought that telling a teacher would be an appropriate response. All the students agreed that walking away was a responsible way of dealing with that situation.

Then I invited the student who was originally playing the bullied character to try an alternative way of dealing with the situation, one he saw his peers do or something else. He chose to say nothing and walk away.

"Now switch roles," I said as I gestured for the student playing the bully to sit in the seat. Transitioning from the bully role to the seat appeared difficult for this student. He looked upset when he sat down, and I allowed a downbeat in my fast-paced facilitation for him to process this transition.

"Put your head in the toilet, ha ha ha," laughed the smaller student, now in the role of the bully. There was a nonthreatening quality to his portrayal of the bully, which I interpreted as being rooted in his discomfort playing that less familiar role. Because it is common for people to become accustomed to playing certain roles in their daily life, role reversals in dramatic enactment are an opportunity for participants to expand their role repertoire and understand different perspectives.

The student originally portraying the bully but now in the bullied role was far less expressive. He appeared withdrawn and I asked him if he could speak out loud the thoughts running through the head of somebody getting bullied. He didn't want to do it, so I solicited the group for ideas. Students spoke about feeling nervous, angry, and powerless.

All this happened in an Oakland middle school class for students diagnosed with learning disabilities. Bullying is a big issue for these youth. It can include physical harm and threats, like those in the role-play, or social exclusion. Often those who are bullied find themselves repeatedly targeted and the physical hurt can be accompanied by psychological harm ranging from depression to suicidal thoughts. Bullying also takes its toll on bullies, who often experience diminished success in school and later at work (Klass, 2009).

According to Maslow's (1943) hierarchy of needs, students need safety and belonging before they can successfully engage in problem solving and critical thinking. Few youth are already safe and secure enough in their developmental need for social acceptance to see bullying for what it is and call out peers who are perpetrating abusive behaviors. Role-playing the different characters in bullying situations illuminates students' individual relationship to bullying. It not only allows bullies and the bullied to examine such abuse but also provides opportunities for bystanders, the majority of youth in most bullying situations, to imagine their role in preventing bullying. Dramatic arts create an opportunity to leverage student understanding and develop self-assertion and confidence.

This example of role-playing shows how dramatic arts can help students develop habits of mind (Hetland, Winner, Veenema, & Sheridan, 2007) that contribute to their overall success in school. Students in the bullying role play "stretched and explored" as they switched roles and began to "observe" phenomenon from perspectives other than their own. As Hetland et al. (2007) write:

> When teachers encourage students to stretch and explore, they do not tell students exactly what to do. Instead, through the level of challenge in the tasks teachers set for students and through the responses teachers make as students work on those tasks, they urge students to experiment, to discover what happens, to play around, and to try out alternatives. (p. 74)

Stretching, exploring, and observing led students to reflect on their responsibilities in bullying situations and develop other ways to respond.

In the rest of this chapter, I describe similar uses of the arts, particularly drama and music—hip-hop specifically—to develop habits of mind in middle school students so they create and participate in positive school learning environments. These examples can be part of the everyday life of a classroom where management is about student understanding as teacher authority.

I draw on my experience as an artist who facilitates aesthetic dialogue on critical social issues. I integrate theater of the oppressed, drama therapy, and elements of hip-hop culture into social healing through drama. My teaching methodology is rooted in my work as a community artist.

Currently, I work at the Buena Vista School, within the Alameda County Juvenile Justice Center, as the arts-integration specialist, where I coach teachers and teaching artists to develop units on character-based literacy through arts-integrated lessons. I have completed collaborative arts-integrated units with math, science, social studies, and English teachers. I organize this chapter according to four principles I use in my work: playful interventions, interpreting metaphors, excluding exclusivity, and challenging a climate of complacency.

PLAYFUL INTERVENTIONS

When using drama to build classroom community and deepen student understanding across disciplines, a playful creative spirit is essential in the classroom. Playful creativity promotes the kind of stretching and exploring portrayed in the opening vignette. It allows students to take on new roles and perspectives, learn from mistakes, and develop understanding that goes beyond initial thinking. This playful spirit best develops through appropriate warm-up activities where feedback is formative and students have opportunities to reflect on where such playfulness leads in their thinking. These activities must also be built on a base of trust and safety.

Trust and safety are paramount in classes integrating drama. As Garbarino, Dubrow, Kostelny, and Pardo (1992) note, especially for children in urban schools, "What has been destroyed . . . is the idea of home, school, and community as a safe place" (p. 83). Inevitably, students will test the limits of what is permitted in the seemingly less structured format of drama. The limit testing may come out physically, for example, a student getting in another student's personal space, or it may come out emotionally in the content of improvisations. Testing threatens safety and ultimately creative playfulness.

You can demonstrate the safety of the class by setting limits to prevent physical or emotional harm like hitting, inappropriate touching, or bigoted put-downs. And when danger is not attached to a potentially inappropriate student action, you can intervene playfully and in the same creative spirit of stretching and exploring.

For example, during a role-play in which young teens were talking back to their parents, the students began speaking over each other and their movements started getting aggressive toward the student playing the parental figure. I was concerned that this might be too much for the student in the parental role, as he was backing away and appeared nervous. I stepped into the scene, using my real authority as a teacher, and "role-played" an authority figure. I stood on a chair and wagged my finger at the students. "What's wrong with you?" There was a silent downbeat. One student stepped over to me and said, "You never let us have any fun!" With exaggerated seriousness I replied, "Is life just fun and games to you?" That was all it took to enroll myself as the antagonist. The students lined up and one by one vented their frustration toward authority in a playful, improvised dialogue with my character.

This intense scene ended in roaring laughter, at which point I stepped down from the chair and invited the students into a circle to reflect as a group on what happened for them in the last scene. Many students reported that they had had fun. This was important for the students because it allowed them to express the animosity they were feeling toward authority (a common characteristic of early adolescent development, especially among the young people with whom I work) without having to engage in a "real" power struggle with me. I was also able to intervene and take the heat off the student who was in the parental role without stopping the play.

By holding space for and playing with the students' resistance to authority, we let everything out on the table without my shutting down their expression or inappropriately colluding with the students against their parents. As Emunah (1994) writes, "The dramatization of actual emotion or behavior, particularly when exaggerated, tends to promote a sense of acceptance and acknowledgement, cathartic release, an atmosphere of playfulness and humor, and a capacity to observe oneself in action" (pp. 86–87).

Clear instructions and routines are the best preventive measures against problematic student behaviors that emerge during confusing, difficult, or drastic transitions in between classroom activities. When using drama in nondrama classes, the drama activities themselves are a break from routine and you may find yourself reluctant to use drama, anticipating that it will create challenging classroom management situations. Setting up routines when you sequence the drama activities appropriately prevents students from getting off task.

Many students are overcoming some form of trauma, such as from violence in the community or at home, yet even then, a sense of playfulness and students' own music as a springboard can lead to productive classroom environments for learning. As Garbarino et al. (1992) point out, "For most children, healing childhood trauma depends on the strength of adult-child relationships. Few children can do the job on their own: the challenges are too great, their resources too few. Teachers . . . must be prepared to hear the children tell their stories in and on their own terms. . . . This acceptance of the child's reality is the starting point for the healing process" (p. 202). I meet the students on their terms, where they are, then join them in their learning process. Music is a useful tool for starting this healing process because young people tell their stories about what they are experiencing in a form that is part of their culture.

Hypervigilance, agitation, and "spacing out" are all common symptoms of posttraumatic stress that I see in my classroom. When a student entered my classroom teasing a classmate aggressively, I asked her, "What's going on with you today?" She deflected my question and responded, "She started it!"

Knowing she needed space to process what she was thinking as well as firm limits on that space, I said, "Let's make a deal; I'll let you pick the warm-up activity if you participate with all of yourself and drop the issue with her for this class period at least."

"Anything I want?" she replied with a mischievous look on her face.

"The rules still apply," I said with a smile. She decided that she wanted to listen to 2pac's "Thugz Mansion," a hip-hop song about what happens after death. The other students agreed; among them was the young woman with whom she had been feuding. I had a feeling that this song was going to speak what was happening under the surface.

As the song played, three students cried, including the two who had been in conflict. After the song was done, I asked the students, "What does this song mean to you?" The two girls who entered the room in conflict shared that they had both lost loved ones recently as a result of street violence. Creating space in the classroom for students to share life experiences that were preoccupying their thoughts was, in this case, successful at defusing a conflict that students were ready to escalate.

This experience brought the classroom community closer together. Had I been more punitive in my approach to the student conflict, the girls may not have opened up and the class would have missed out on this opportunity to dialogue and develop understanding about death and street violence. I met the students where they were, they understood themselves and others' lives more deeply, and we were able to continue with class.

INTERPRETING METAPHORS

Do you ever ask yourself, "What is going on in my classroom?" This critical question is best kept open-ended for ongoing inquiry. Continuously reinvestigating and reinterpreting your classroom dynamics will help you better understand what is going on with your students so you can target classroom activities to meet students exactly where they are.

I remember trying to get a group of students into a role-play for their social studies class where I was working as a teaching artist collaborating on an arts-integration unit with their social studies teacher. I gave instructions for the group to rearrange the space for the role-play. The students remained seated, most with blank stares and the others looking around to see if any of their peers were going to follow my instructions. This is the point where I needed to keep my interpretation open. It's easy to become frustrated and think, "Why aren't they obeying my directions?" In this case I took a more open approach. I named the behavior and asked the class about it. "When I gave that instruction, nobody responded. What's going on?" I said, attempting not to sound condescending or rhetorical.

You may be thinking, "If the class did not respond to the instructions, why would they respond to a question like that?" I thought to myself about the possible reasons why the class would exhibit this behavior; then I said, "Raise your hand if you haven't had anything to eat today." Most of the students raised their hands and the energy of the class took on a more expressive tone. I spoke to their situation in that moment. Unfortunately, many students in that class do not eat anything until lunch. Even without eating, however, the students' focus seemed to increase. Imagine what food could have done in that moment. The students' inattention to my directions was not only about food. Food was the metaphor I chose to use in this situation. They appeared to have low energy. Food is an external source of energy, an external culprit for a problem that I learned more about as I continued to reinterpret the metaphor of student behavior in that class. Over time I grew to associate the students' behavior with what I call a climate of complacency, discussed later in this chapter.

Students need to be part of interpreting the classroom metaphors, and drama can help them develop this skill. It is critical to open space in the class for students to stretch and explore within dramatic realms and play with new ideas. Such openness requires students and especially teachers to relax their desire to make meaning quickly without observation, reflection, or stretching and exploring.

An activity I like to use to stretch and explore in this way is Complete the Image. In a pair, two students make the first image as both freeze in a statue. One of the partners changes his or her position in relation to the other and the activity continues with each partner changing position and creating new images with evolving meanings.

A variation can also be played in circle with the whole class. One student stands in the middle of the circle as a statue. Another student enters the circle and places his or her body in relationship to the first student. The first student holds the pose then steps out of the middle, making way for the next student to enter and complete a new image. Sometimes I call this activity "an image is worth a thousand words" and we play in silence focusing on our body language. This activity, done to develop the habit of mind of stretch and explore, is also a useful warm-up for an extended version, which I call DJing Images.

DJing Images is similar to Boal's (1992) Orchestra and the Conductor (p. 96) and Emunah's (1994) Emotional Orchestra (p. 159). The DJ conducts the group as if mixing records. We warm up with Complete the Image. Next we brainstorm single words or phrases representing a feeling or issue relevant to the topic of the class. Sometimes, when the group theme is familiar to the students, I skip this step and use words and phrases that come from student writing or group discussions.

After the class chooses or I select one of the words, they sculpt themselves to create a group image or statue of the word. The class holds an image for at least 5 seconds in silence, and then I announce the next word or phrase.

When the group strikes a poignant image, ask everyone to hold that image, take a deep breath, and saturate their minds with the inner voice of their statue. I continue by announcing, "When I say, 'Go,' you're going to speak your sculpture's inner monologue, like a free write where your pen doesn't leave the paper. Keep your tongue speaking until I say, 'Stop.'" When I tell the students to stop, I remind them to take a deep breath. I then ask them to take the essential nugget of truth or insight from what they just said—a word, sound, or short phrase—and repeat that essential bit over and over when I say, "Go." The students repeat their phrase until told to stop. For the third round, I ask them to add a short, repetitive movement to accompany their essential word, phrase, or sound. When I say, "Stop," this time, I instruct them to hold their position. I put on instrumental music, usually with hip-hop beats. I continue on to the fourth round, saying, "Time to DJ this image. When I tap you, do your sound and movement once then return to your still image." I tap people in rhythm with the beat and try to tap people multiple times and play with different juxtapositions. I invite students to take turns playing my role as DJ. This activity continues through more of the words and phrases from our brainstorm. When we get to another image worth exploring, we repeat the process, starting at the stage of listening to the sculpture's inner voice.

When we debrief the activity, we begin to explore meaning and interpret metaphors. I use discussion with the whole class. Writing can also support interpreting the metaphor. Capturing images with a digital camera and displaying them in the classroom can make students' learning visible and support deeper observation and further meaning making.

DJing Images can be used to support learning in a variety of subject areas. In science, students can explore a local ecosystem by taking on the roles of plants, animals, water, and rocks. In social studies, they can examine a current event or theme relevant to history. For example, invite students to create an image of war and then an image of peace. Was one image more difficult to make than the other? Why? In math, students can focus on rhythm by moving to a 4 count then freezing for a 4, 8 count, then freezing for 8, 16, 32, 64, and so on. This progression supports the concept of exponential growth. Repeating the sequence in reverse demonstrates exponential decay. Finally, this activity can be part of a physical education class as students use drama and movement to warm up their bodies and their minds.

EXCLUDING EXCLUSIVITY: COOPERATIVE PLAY
FOR INCLUSIVE CLASS CULTURE

Were you friends with all your classmates in school? I wasn't, and it's no mystery that youth choose to socialize with some of their peers and not others. Unfortunately, young people, preteens, in particular, are sensitive to social inclusion and exclusion. For some students who are the target of bullying and ridicule, social issues can dominate their attention, making it hard to focus on anything else. Knowing that this is the social situation in many schools, there are drama activities you can use in your class to develop a more socially inclusive class culture. Drama is a great way to develop a healthy group dynamic in the classroom, which will in turn reduce behavioral problems while increasing student engagement. In the following paragraphs, I've included a few simple drama activities to "exclude exclusivity" and promote a positive, inclusive classroom culture.

One Leader and One Guesser

One student, the "guesser," steps out of the room and the teacher and the rest of the students determine who the leader will be. The rest of the students, in unison, then follow whatever gestures—marching in place, swinging an arm, shrugging shoulders—the leader initiates. When the guesser returns to the room, he or she tries to determine which student is leading the class. The leader is encouraged to switch up the gesture regularly instead of only doing one movement the whole time. This activity is a fun way to cultivate observation as a habit of mind, for both the guesser and the other participants who need to focus on the ever-changing movements they are mirroring. The use of unison movement and guessing provide a structure that reduces any potential performance anxiety that students may feel.

French Telephone/Group Mirror

This activity is borrowed from Emunah (1994, p. 154). Ask everyone to form a circle and put one arm up with a finger pointing to the sky. Lower your arm to point at someone in the circle. Now that person points at someone who hasn't been pointed at yet. Continue until everyone has been pointed at. The last person points back to you. Tell everybody to look at the person he or she pointed at, not the person who pointed at them. Tell them to take a deep breath, relax, and get a blank look on their faces. When you say, "Go," everyone should mirror the person he or she is looking at, including every subtle movement, even twitches. Students should try displaying a variety of facial expressions.

While this activity is about observation, it also develops skills in expression and physically challenges students to stretch and explore a variety of movements. Again, this activity can relieve performance anxiety because it is a whole-group activity, which means that no particular student is in the spotlight. Through reflecting and amplifying gestures, students somatically express and personify each other's physical state, which builds group cohesion, connection, and even empathy. It can be quite funny as well. Laughter and fun help students develop positive regard for one another and develop the most valuable asset a group can have—love.

Blind Walk with Sound

One student leads another blindfolded student by a sound that they develop together at the start of the activity. This exercise requires auditory observation and trust. The inherent challenge of following a sound without looking requires that students stretch and explore with their senses. The responsibility of leading requires that students consider their partner by leading in a way that creates a challenge that is still achievable. This game makes an ideal warm-up for Sound Gates.

Sound Gates

Half the class pairs up to create sound gates. The pairs link their arms in the air and make a sound in unison. The other half of the class closes their eyes and walks through the gates by following the sounds. This activity requires similar habits of mind as Blind Walk with Sound, with an additional layer of observation by the students acting as the sound gates. What strategies can they observe students using to navigate the sound gates without looking?

Advice Game

Three students role play "experts" giving advice: one good, one bad, and one horrible. The person seeking advice chooses which advice to take. You can use this activity in many ways, since it is a structure that takes well to a wide range of content. Use it to review subject matter, problem-solve an issue in the class, or explore new subject matter while initially assessing the students' understanding in that subject area. Depending on the subject area and your purpose, you may want to use different categories of advice.

Playing games like the ones just described enhances student engagement, builds trust among students and teachers, and provides creative opportunities to express and assess student understanding. Creating opportunities for students to participate in group cooperative activities and physical games breaks isolation and the sense of monotony that can set the stage for cliques, exclusivity, and behavioral problems. Facilitating group processes that generate a positive, inclusive environment is essential for creating a classroom where students are invested in class, love, learning, and liberation.

CHALLENGING A CLIMATE OF COMPLACENCY

Ask students to step out from their desks? That sounds like a risky proposition. What will the students do without the familiar order and structure of a desk? Wouldn't it be easier to manage the classroom if I just did seated activities? I hear these concerns from teachers when I enter their classrooms to collaborate on dramatic arts. It's true. If students are not used to getting out of their desks and interacting with one another, drama will be a change and a challenge. Some students may express initial resistance to the change in routine and structure. Some may resist the challenge to the climate of complacency, as group dramatic processes require interpersonal demands that do not exist when students sit passively at a desk. These are legitimate concerns, so address them. "Today we are going to do something different, and I know it's not what you're used too. It may seem weird to you, but if you take a risk and step outside your comfort zone a little, we can have a lot of fun and learn."

I have also taken to soliciting advice from more experienced students to ease the transition into drama and get students out of their complacency. "Raise your hand if you have experience acting or if you've ever done a play before." Then I ask students who raised their hands to offer advice to students who have never acted before. "What would have been helpful for you to hear before going into your first drama experience?" This question is great way to solicit leadership within the class. Middle and older elementary students may also take the advice of peers with more weight than that of a teacher.

Games that include making loud noise and moving around tend to break through the spell of disengagement and passivity just by their nature. The more regularly you integrate cooperative and interactive activities into your classroom practice, the more engaging your class will be. If you start the school year off with drama exercises focused on developing teamwork, and continue using drama activities as a part of your daily or weekly routine, you will notice a reduction in student apathy. Choose activities and exercises that are also engaging to you. Teachers can become complacent and apathetic too. Refresh your passion routinely by sharing in creative acts with your students.

CONCLUSION

Many "behavioral problems" can be transformed and rechanneled by providing creative outlets in the classroom. Do you have students in your class who could be referred to as drama queens or drama kings? Explicitly put them in that role and see what happens. Developing an inclusive and supportive classroom culture through drama exercises increases student engagement and reduces interpersonal conflicts that emerge when no energy is spent on team building.

All art forms can be used to build a positive classroom environment for learning. Because drama is particularly immediate and communal, however, it makes an ideal medium for exploring social, emotional, and intellectual issues in the classroom. To embody and express understanding requires a deeper knowing that any multiple-choice question can assess. By facilitating relevant and challenging interactive drama processes in your class you are creating opportunities for students who may not feel as comfortable on paper as in person to thrive. Drama allows students, in essence, to make their learning visible to themselves and others. Integrating drama may be hard at first for you and the students, so don't give up. One of the best gifts you can give your students and yourself is permission to make mistakes. Model it, rehearse it, and act on it.

REFERENCES

Boal, A. (1992). *Games for actors and non-actors*. London: Routledge.

Emunah, R. (1994). *Acting for real: Drama therapy process, technique, and performance*. New York: Routledge.

Garbarino, J., Dubrow, N., Kostelny, K., & Pardo, C. (1992). *Children in danger*. San Francisco: Jossey-Bass.

Hetland, L., Winner, E., Veenema, S., & Sheridan, K. (2007). *Studio thinking: The real benefits of visual arts education*. New York: Teachers College Press.

Klass, P. (2009, 9 June). At last, facing down bullies (and their enablers). *New York Times*. Retrieved June 9, 2009, from http://www.nytimes.com/2009/06/09/health/09klas.html?em

Maslow, A. (1943). A theory of human motivation. *Psychological Review, 50*(4), 370–396.

CHAPTER 10

Keeping Reading and Writing Personal and Powerful

Bringing Poetry Writing and Bookmaking Together

Cathleen Micheaels

WHETHER YOU ARE a new or veteran teacher, arts educator or artist, if you reflect on your own most powerful learning experiences—the learning experiences that opened you up to new understanding, that connected you to the larger universe, that changed your life—surely, they were not the hours you spent filling in the blanks on worksheets. Rather, they were the kind of impassioned *aha* moments when someone or something inspired you, when you felt that who you were and what you had discovered and perhaps even articulated or created mattered in this world. For me, language and books are at the heart of my life-changing learning experiences and what I believe should be a central part of every child's learning experience.

As much as this chapter is focused on bringing the art of writing together with the art of making books in the classroom and school community, it is also about the role of teaching with passion. This goes beyond just caring about students and their academic success to wanting students to be transformed by the learning process, to experience school not as a series of instructions and tests but as a window on a whole world of discoveries and possibilities. And poetry writing and bookmaking are among the most immediate and important ways in, particularly in elementary school classrooms where learning to read and write are so central and critical.

LEARNING AND TEACHING ARE PERSONAL

What do you remember about learning to read and write? Did your teachers instill in you a love or a fear of language? Was learning to read and write like a window opening up or like a door that seemed forever slammed shut? Do you remember how you had to struggle and practice when you were first learning to read and write? Do you remember the first book that you loved reading? Do you remember the first time you were really engaged in the process of writing? Asking yourself to think back on your own experiences as a student never fails to reveal an important and sometimes forgotten and very personal part of your own educational history—a powerful and not necessarily always positive experience that likely still informs your own practice as an educator.

I recall a missed learning opportunity that took place in elementary school when we were first introduced to the solar system. Seeing the planets from afar literally changed me and how I perceived my place in this world. I still have the 10 mimeographed pages of text that we were given to read and number—one long, slender column of text accompanied by illustrations we were asked to color in with crayons:

> Why do planets keep
> traveling around the sun,
> instead of racing straight
> off into space? The reason is
> gravity. . . .
> Why don't all the planets
> get pulled into the sun?
> . . . The earth, for
> example, is racing around the
> sun at a speed of 64,800
> miles an hour! Think of the
> force with which the earth is
> trying to pull away from the sun.

Remarkably, the language reads almost like a poem in some places. I think now on a subconscious level that must certainly be why the text made such an impression on me and why I have kept the pages all these years.

Sadly, none of the wonder, none of the expansion of my understanding of my place in the universe that I remember experiencing when we were studying the planets was translated into any kind of *visible learning* or opportunity to "find the meaning" of or reflect on what I had encountered and experienced (Rinaldi, 2001, p. 79). I can't help but wonder now what would have happened if I had been asked to write a poem, an ode, say, to Saturn or Pluto, my then two favorite planets (although the latter is no longer officially a planet). Or, if I had been given the opportunity and permission to delve further into the questions that studying space, gravity, planets, and comets conjured up for me—questions about God, infinity, and what happens when life ends. The way, for example, a teacher and I did together years later with a class of fifth graders in San Francisco who were studying the universe as part of a schoolwide partnership focused on integrating writing across the curriculum. Here's an example of one of the poems that came out of that kind of reflecting written by one of the students:

Emptiness
Before the darkness, before the cold
there was a time when the beginning of
history was only a start then became bigger
and bigger things. Planets, night, dreams
and emptiness like space, tons
of space, space that you couldn't think of
using up, it just sits there, it's something
that I'll never understand. Why is it there?

I also wonder what kind of visual representation I would have come up with if my teacher had introduced my class to using oil pastels on art paper the way a fifth-grade teacher and reading specialist did as part of a project designed to give students a chance to explore what they had learned about space through writing odes and creating companion images as part of a triptych, or three-fold, book. I can't recall ever making a book during all my years in school, and although we did have an enthusiastic band and glee club teacher, arts experiences at my elementary school were otherwise limited to the same holiday-themed coloring, cutting, and pasting of turkeys, candy canes, and leprechauns that you may still sometimes come across on bulletin boards in the school where you work.

LITERARY ARTS AND LANGUAGE ARTS

The literary arts, specifically poetry, are often not thought of or included as part of the arts—the visual and performing arts of dance, music, theater, and visual arts (drawing, painting, printmaking, and sculpture). Even within circles of arts educators I am more often than not surprised that the literary arts are left out. Part of this comes out of how the literary arts (poetry, in particular) are and are not valued within our culture, and part of this comes out of how they are taught in our schools. In most public schools the literary arts—reading and writing poems, stories, personal essays, or nonfiction—are crammed into the teaching of language arts, which has become almost entirely focused on teaching the mechanics of reading and writing and not necessarily on the love, joy, or art of those two endeavors. Almost every teacher I know loves the literary arts and wants to spend more time in class on them, but, not surprisingly, not all teachers grasp how to teach poetry or feel comfortable doing so—a situation that is even more pronounced in schools where the pressure of increasing test scores weighs heavily on the minds of administrators, teachers, and students. In the case of poetry writing, textbooks and curriculum resources often resort to poor examples and simplistic approaches to engaging students in writing their own poems.

There is a rich opportunity for both teachers and students in looking at the literary arts and poetry in particular through a cultural and historical lens, understanding poets as artists; as profound thinkers; and in some cases, such as that of Pablo Neruda or Langston Hughes, as the public voice of a particular time and place in history that remains relevant and powerful decades, even centuries, later. Consider, for example, the poems written by Langston Hughes, who was part of that vibrant community of artists and thinkers that so powerfully shaped that place and time now known as the Harlem Renaissance. Take for instance that opening line of one of his most famous poems, "Harlem [2]," "What happens to a dream deferred?" (Hughes, 1994, p. 426). The ten lines that follow take hold of our attention through a series of metaphors—"a sore," "rotten meat," "a syrupy sweet" and "a heavy load"—which make us *see* and *feel* the forceful answer to his question.

Poems offer us an insight into our connection to both the known past and the unknown future, offer us a way to give voice to our deepest expressions of love, pain, joy, beauty, injustice, peace, and brutality. Poems are often the art form people turn to at moments of great life transition—commencement ceremonies, inaugurations, marriages, births, deaths—and yet they are an art with which many people are not very familiar.

Good partnerships and good curriculum are essential to arriving at powerful arts integration and learning through poetry writing. But I would argue that without understanding the arts experience firsthand, without allowing the experience to become personal—reading aloud poems written by published poets and looking closely at the poetic devices they employ—without writing in an in-class setting within a limited time frame and then reading the poem aloud, without that practice of *developing craft, stretching and exploring, engaging and persisting,* or what Hetland, Winner, Veenema, and Sheridan (2007) describe as the "habits of mind" that come out of the actual experience, without all this, the teacher misses perhaps the most important elements of poetry writing.

HOW MAKING BOOKS TRANSFORMS WRITTEN WORDS

Before we move too much further into how poetry writing and bookmaking can be brought together to transform teaching and learning . . . why bookmaking?

Books, like poems, share a long-standing and honored role in our common humanity. Bookmaking not only offers a beautiful framework in which students can make public their own writing but also offers classroom teachers a very manageable way to guide students in an art with a long and powerful history. Bookmaking is a profoundly political act that was revolutionized and democratized in the 1400s by Johannes Gutenberg, who created movable foundry type and the earliest printing press—an act that has been perhaps even more radically revolutionized and democratized in the past 2 decades with the increasingly available and affordable technology of the personal computer and home printer.

Writing poems alone is powerful, but what is even more so is giving weight to them—making them concrete and visible in books. Books transform writing into something physical, and this process of putting words into books is a gratifying and extremely effective way to motivate emerging writers. As book artist and educator Edward H. Hutchins (2008) notes in answering his own question, Why make books? "Put simply, the book arts are at the intersection where writing, illustration, discovery, creativity and sharing come together to support the classroom curriculum."

As with poetry writing, actually experiencing the process of making books is critical for teachers in bringing bookmaking into the classroom—understanding firsthand how folding paper into an accordion spine of mountains and valleys can get confusing, how glue sticks are not a very effective adhesive without applying pressure, or how a beautiful book can be constructed out of the most basic and affordable materials. What is remarkable for most teachers to discover is just how manageable making books is in the classroom and how well making books supports learning in all subjects, particularly writing.

ASKING QUESTIONS, MAKING DISCOVERIES

Before we move on to two specific examples of how poetry writing and bookmaking can be brought together in the classroom, let's look a little closer at the process of writing poems.

Maybe, like many teachers, parents, or other educators I have worked with, you have participated in workshops or professional development sessions focused on poetry writing. Perhaps, like them, even after you have loosened up with a pre-writing activity and amazed yourself with the results, you have felt uncomfortable when asked to write a poem because you do not really consider yourself a writer. Maybe you find it difficult to come up with anything meaningful to say in a limited time. Then, after sitting with your unease for 5 or 10 minutes, helped along perhaps by an idea drawn from one of the model poems or the person next to you, you started to write. This experience of pushing through the discomfort or *engaging and persisting* is important for us to experience as adult learners so that we can remember firsthand how struggling with a skill or concept is a necessary part of the learning process and, therefore, understand better how to help our students.

One of the reasons I am so drawn to the concept of writing poems that ask questions is that they offer an important opportunity to understand the value of working away from what is known toward what is discovered in the process of writing. Poems that ask questions can arrive at literal, factual, or metaphorical answers or can be answered with questions as in Langston Hughes's poem "Harlem [2]." If you've read any amount of modern and contemporary poetry, one thing you've likely noticed is that poets ask a lot of questions in their poems.

So, let's try doing just that—either on your own or with a few of your colleagues. First, pass out two sets of index cards in different colors (three of each color if you are trying this with a few colleagues and five of each color if you're on your own). On one set or color of cards write down three (or five) big and perhaps not so big life questions—questions you may have asked when you were 5 and may still be asking when you are 50. Think of questions about life (love, existence, death, beauty, or why there is prejudice or hatred), about science (stars, clouds, or microorganisms), or social science (about the meaning of community or the Bill of Rights). Then on the second set or color of cards, write the answers to your questions. Collect the questions in one box and the answers in another, and read one randomly selected card from each box. Or simply place all the cards, writing side up, on a table, randomly pick up one of the question color cards and see what happens when you match the question with one and then another of the answer color cards.

I have brought this same pre-writing exercise into many classrooms and professional development sessions and never fail to be surprised by the results of how juxtaposing two seemingly disparate ideas or objects—in this case a mismatched question and answer—together yield such powerful and sometimes delightful and humorous discoveries. This concept of juxtaposition is an important element of poetry and perhaps most significantly of the haiku poem—a form which does not really translate well from Japanese to English (Akmakjian, 1980, p. 35), and which (not unlike teaching and learning) lies finally not in a strict adherence to rules but in the artful calling attention to first this object, observation, or moment, then placing that next to another object, observation or moment to reveal something deeper, surprising, and more resonant.

After you've had a chance to experience the process of making discoveries through the pre-writing experience of juxtaposition, select one question and one answer or one question and several answers or a series of related question-answer pairs and try writing a poem that is 6 to 12 lines long that uses the questions and answers you selected and on which you work for no more than 20 minutes (about the time normally available to students who are asked to write poems in the classroom).

When I'm working with students and teachers in the classroom, we always start by reading aloud and looking together at a model poem or two. In this case, we read poems that ask questions, including "Harlem [2]," and take a look at what we notice or *observe* about how Hughes uses juxtaposition, metaphor, voice, enjambment, and line breaks in that brilliantly short and yet remarkably large poem. As the emphasis here is on bringing poetry writing together with bookmaking, we also look at model books, in this case, accordion slat books—simple folded books with eight sections that are longer than wide and when folded up resemble the "slat" of a fence—that have poems that ask questions transcribed

Figure 10.1. First grader making an ode slat book.

onto the slat pages. We again notice or *observe* the parts of the slat book—two covered covers, an eight-slat-page spine and simple ribbon at both ends to keep the book closed. Looking at the model book *before* we start reading and writing poems is a critical element, as seeing the model book helps us to *envision* how our completed poems will come together in a finished book. For students who are not particularly comfortable with writing, this is especially important, as the book is often what most excites them about (or provides them a way into) the process of writing a poem.

One reason I continue to love the idea of asking questions is not only because the results are so endlessly new and surprising but also because it provides an immediate way to draw on prior knowledge across subject areas. The example that follows, written by a teacher just starting her career, is testament to how much can be discovered through a 10-minute pre-writing experience followed by 20 minutes of quiet and concentrated *reflection* and *expression*:

Ambition
What is the shape of morning?
The arch of the cat's back
Stretching at the door,
The full, rounded aromas
Of mama's breakfast in the kitchen,
The stripes of dawn's light
Filtered through the drapes,
Wavering on the ceiling.

What gets me out of bed?
Fear of a wasted life.

BRINGING POETRY WRITING AND BOOKMAKING TOGETHER

The following two examples and reflections, like the previous example of asking big and not so big life questions, are drawn from years of experience working with students, teachers, and families in public elementary and middle schools, primarily in California but also in the Midwest and the metropolitan New York City area. They are included not as plans of how to carry out actual arts-integrated teaching but as illustrations of what is possible, as concrete examples of arts integration through poetry writing and bookmaking. They come out of collaboration with teachers, students, and families, as well as other artists and teaching artists in diverse educational communities. They have been adapted and refined and will continue to be based on what we together continue to learn from writing poems and making books that are connected to learning across subject areas.

All these examples involved some combination of three basic components: hands-on professional development and coaching, classroom modeling and partnering, and reflection on the teaching and learning process. All used adaptations of three invaluable works on teaching frameworks and resources developed by Project Zero at Harvard University's Graduate School of Education: *Teaching for Understanding* (Blythe, 1997), *Studio Thinking* (Hetland et al., 2007), and *Making Learning Visible* (Rinaldi, 2001). Finally, all were brought into the classroom in developmentally appropriate steps that provided students opportunities to draw on prior knowledge, innovate and struggle with new concepts and skills, apply learning in other subject areas, and challenge expectations of what they can accomplish.

ODE TO AN ODE

The idea of writing odes inspired by the great Chilean poet Pablo Neruda is not new, and perhaps a few of you have even taught the ode before. I have always loved Neruda's poems, which even in translation are so rich and compelling. What Neruda accomplished in his remarkable odes to fruits and vegetables (and other ordinary objects like shoes and socks) was to both bring the ode as a poetic form down to earth by celebrating commonplace objects and also lift those objects out of their humble (perhaps even unnoticed and unappreciated) existence through his extraordinary use of language. What really brought the ode home for me, however, was when I realized just how much students connected to the fruits and vegetables in Neruda's odes when they were brought into the classroom—how actually studying the fruits and vegetables, looking at them closely, cutting them in half, tasting them, and researching them, transformed the experience of reading and writing odes.

Figure 10.2. Fourth grader writing an ode to an artichoke.

This revelation came out of a desire to help students *stretch and explore*, to move beyond descriptive language that was obvious and worn out, to ignite in them a passion for discovering new words and see how bringing "ordinary" words together with "extraordinary" words yielded poems that were more tangible and lively, richer and more complex. *Observing* a pomegranate or an artichoke, for instance, helped students make discoveries through language and craft poems that were powerful to read both on the page and aloud, poems that were true to the spirit of fruits and vegetables.

First, I introduce the students to the model book, in this case a slat or a flag book—a pop-up–like book with an accordion-folded spine and three rows of "flags," or pages which criss-cross when the book is opened up—both of which never fail to elicit a few *oohs* when they are opened. We look at all the steps that went into creating the book, from writing the ode to folding the spine to gluing in the pages or, in the case of the flag book, the tricky step of gluing in the nine multicolored flag pages. Then, we dive right into Pablo Neruda and his extraordinary odes.

After learning about Neruda's life, we zero in on one of his odes or an excerpt in classes of younger students. We read the ode aloud and start to notice its attributes: the title, the words, the lines, the length, the voice, where the poem starts and ends, and who or what the poem is addressing. We notice, as for example, in the Stephen Mitchell translation (1997) of perhaps Neruda's most famous fruit or vegetable ode, "Ode to the Watermelon," how the watermelon is revealed to us through rich descriptive language and metaphor ("coolest of all the planets" and "green whale of summer"). Reading the ode aloud together entices us to slice open our own watermelon to find out what is inside ("a flag" and "a waterfall") and what watermelons offer nutritionally, or if we don't have our own watermelon on hand, to look at a color reproduction of the famous Mexican painter Diego Rivera's painting of watermelons. Neruda's ode inspires in us the curiosity and desire to know more.

The ode invites us to think about where and in what season watermelons are grown and also how watermelons are eaten, opportunities for thinking about the voice of the poem, who or what the poem is addressed to, and what language can most fully capture the stature and hidden beauty of the watermelon among all the other fruits ("queen of the fruitshop," "mountain of exquisite food," and "jewel box of water").

In classrooms where Spanish is the primary home language, looking at the ode in its original Spanish alongside its English translation provides a rich opportunity for thinking about the origin of words. In two bilingual classes of third graders, we wrote our own odes to fruits and vegetables in English first and then translated them into Spanish. We connected language development with the studio habit of *observing*. We enlivened the schoolwide nutrition program by making connections to cultural and family traditions. First, we brainstormed, wrote, and rewrote our odes to pineapples and lemons (all part of *developing craft*), then translated the odes into Spanish. We used a simple template modeled after Pablo Neruda's odes to help students learn how to extend description and metaphor. Our template was divided up into eight sections for the eight pages of our books (with younger grades a simpler, scaled-down template is used for making a less involved accordion slat book).

After writing our first draft odes we then transcribed them, first in pencil then in felt pens the color of our fruits, onto paper divided up into sections (both the ode template and page template are copied onto legal-size paper, which is an easier size for students of all ages to manage).

Then we moved into making the book, in this case, the accordion flag book, with pages that seemed to magically crisscross when the covers were opened up. First, we made decorative paste grain papers the colors of the outsides and insides of our fruits to use for our book spines. Paste grain papers are similar to finger-painted papers, made of a non-toxic medium called methylcellulose. Metallic tempera paints are used, and four-sided, notched plastic tile tools make repeated types of lines and patterns (creating a "grain" or texture on the paper's surface). Making paste grain papers reinforces the concept of *drawing on prior knowledge*, as most students are already familiar with the process and materials from early finger painting experiences. Paste grain papers build on the process by introducing students to how to use simple tools (notched tile adhesive spreaders and foam brushes) and materials (nontoxic methylcellulose medium and nontoxic metallic tempera paints) to create beautifully patterned papers while exploring two of the basic elements of art—color and line. Once we had selected a piece of art paper the color of the inside or outside of our fruits, brushed on the pigment medium, and experimented with making different sizes and types of lined patterns that capture the essence of our fruits or

Figure 10.3. Template for writing an ode.

#1

Ode To _____
(name of your fruit or vegetable)

_____
(your name)

#2

Oh, _____, _____
(descriptive word)   (descriptive word)

_____,
(name of your fruit or vegetable)

#3

you are the color of _____
(what fruit or vegetable is the color of)

#4

that _____,
(tell a little more)

#5

you are like _____
(what fruit or vegetable is like)

#6

that _____,
(tell a little more)

#7

native of _____,
(where fruit or vegetable is from)

#8

you give us _____.
(what fruit or vegetable gives us)

vegetables (straight, wavy, woven) with our adhesive spreaders, we let the papers dry. Then, we were ready to learn how to fold our book spines. First we practiced with construction paper, folding our papers into mountains and valleys by matching our corners, making soft then hard folds, creasing the folds, and repeating this until we all had an accordion spine with eight folded slats. Then we repeated the process, this time using our decorative papers. Once our accordion spines were completed we glued our covers to the front and the back slats of our spines.

Now our book was starting to look like a book and we began our next steps, gluing in our nine flag pages (eight pages for the poem sections and one page saved in the middle for an illustration of the fruit). First, we made a gluing mark (or X) so we'd know where to glue our flag pages. This is where the real magic comes in, with the students focusing so intently on gluing their flags in the right place—the top row moving from left to right, the middle row from right to left, and the bottom row back in the left-to-right direction—then suddenly seeing how their completed book structures "worked" just like the model. This step required students to *envision* while also paying careful attention, consulting the model to make sure the pages were in the right order.

Bookmaking invites students to revisit basic art and math concepts such as shape by identifying squares, rectangles, and triangles while folding and gluing and using nonstandard measurement such as "the width of a pinky finger" or "the visual center."

During the process of writing and bookmaking, we learned something new each week about our fruits through tasting fresh, healthy foods made from them.

Figure 10.4. Third graders holding ode flag books.

We *reflected* on what we had learned, making our learning visible. We looked at botanical and graphic representations of our fruits and experimented with making our own illustrations first in pencil and then using art pens. We transcribed our odes onto the flag pages (English on one side and Spanish on the other). All the while we practiced reading our odes aloud in English and Spanish and talked about how we would share our poems and books with other students and teachers at the school and with our families. In between the teachers and students put into practice what we had learned together by writing odes to vegetables, editing and transcribing them onto the computer and making poem broadsides, also using the decorative papers we had made.

The collaboration culminated first with an in-class opportunity to look at our books and broadsides. We read our poems aloud and reflected on what we had learned and accomplished. This was followed by a book exhibit and poetry reading, with families bringing foods made from the fruits and vegetables we had studied and with students welcoming our guests, guiding them through the exhibit, which included photographs and reflections on the learning, and serving refreshments.

Later in the year, the teachers and students revisited the ode, applying what they had learned, by now writing odes to birds. This time the students and teachers came up with their own writing template and broadside design, all inspired by the birds they had been observing outside their classroom windows as part of a yearlong study of the local bird habitat and migration. The students read their odes aloud at a ceremony to mark the end of the school year—a beautiful and symbolic honoring of their transition from third grade into fourth grade.

RECLAIMING THE ACROSTIC

In addition to introducing students and teachers to more formal structures, such as the contemporary ode, and to new ways of approaching the contemporary lyric poem through asking questions, I also like to reintroduce forms with which they are perhaps already familiar. One of these is the acrostic, a poem form that in many classrooms is taught in a simplistic way that neglects to draw on its rich and complex history.

I have not always loved all poems, and I used to actively dislike the acrostic poem. In fact, in fourth grade when we had to write acrostic poems using our names, the whole experience and my finished poem felt forced and untrue:

Curious
Attentive
Thoughtful
Helpful
Listener

Eager
Enthusiastic
Nice

"Ugh." That or a polite silence is the response I often hear from teachers when I now mention the acrostic. What this word list approach often results in is just that—a list of words that somewhat but not entirely capture something true about a person, object, or feeling. While this take on the acrostic does introduce the idea of puzzling out the "right" words, the result is not really a poem but rather the skeleton of a poem.

The truth is that the acrostic has a rich history and offers students a remarkable opportunity to learn about line lengths and breaks and coming upon the unexpected turn in a poem. And now I love bringing acrostic poems into classrooms. I love them because like books they have spines (the acrostic words) and hidden hearts. I love them because they encourage inventive word choice. I love them because they are such perfect companion poems for the pendant or necklace book—a simple variation of an accordion book that almost every teacher or student I have ever worked with immediately wants to make. The pendant book is a small amulet-like book and so the written text or visual images that work best with it are also small. The acrostic poem using a single word as its key or spine word—rather than two or three words—fits quite well on the pages inside the pendant book.

"The most common acrostic," Preminger (1965) tells us, "is a poem in which the initial letters of each line have a meaning when read downward," but there are many variations including poem and prose compositions "in which the initial

Figure 10.5. Simple acrostic pendant books.

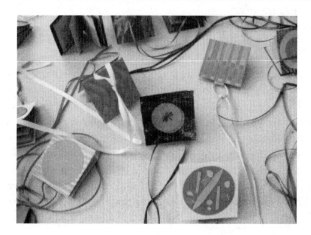

letters of each paragraph make up the word or words in question, [that] use the middle (mesostich) or the final letter (telestich) of each line or with the key letters distributed by stanzas and not by lines" (p. 4). "According to some, the acrostic was first used as a mnemotechnic device to ensure completeness in the oral transmission of sacred texts. In ancient times mystical significance was attributed to acrostic compositions . . . During the Middle Ages the acrostic often spelled out the name of the author or a saint. Later also the name of the patron or the beloved was thus designated" (Preminger, 1965, p. 4). This history is important in understanding the appropriate approach and subject for the acrostic and helps us understand why acrostics that are written about a treasured object, idea, or person are the most compelling.

Here is an example of an acrostic poem written by a seventh-grade student about her relationship with her twin sister that I like to use as a model:

Twin
Together
With my sister I was born.
In my mother
Never did we part.

I love this acrostic for the haiku-like simplicity of its language and its subtle turn— for being everything that that acrostic that so many of us had to write in elementary school is not. Below is another example of an acrostic written by a mother who participated in a recent family arts day of writing poems and making books with her (coincidently) twin eleven year-old daughters.

Aria
Awaited, longed for
Right below my heart,
Inseparable, entwined in spirit, my daughters
Arrived: Ariane/Mariah, song of my heart.

In classes where we are writing acrostics, we start with a pre-writing exercise using an index card—this time only one card—on which everyone was asked to write three things that held a special meaning for them on the front. Then they selected the one word that resonated with them the most and wrote that word on the back of the index card. Then they thought of three more specific or descriptive words that the original word called up. This is an important step and is similar to that of looking at the actual fruits and vegetables when writing the ode, because it pushes beyond the first and perhaps general and worn-out word toward the more specific and personally meaningful word, putting into practice the studio habit of mind *expressing*.

MAKING A PLACE FOR POETRY AND BOOKMAKING IN THE CLASSROOM

By now, I am hoping you are thinking about how writing poems and making books offers possibilities for bringing the arts and arts integration into teaching and learning. Secretly, I am hoping that you are already planning to do this despite all the requirements and mandates that make doing so seem so impossible. The first step is allowing yourself and your students the permission and opportunity. This is often what takes the most courage and tenacity, given the reality of what many of our public schools face—this inviting in and making a place for art and artful thinking, teaching, and learning in the classroom.

REFERENCES

Akmakjian, H. (1980). *Snow falling from a bamboo leaf: The art of haiku.* Santa Barbara, CA: Capra Press.

Blythe, T. (1997). *The teaching for understanding guide.* San Francisco: Jossey-Bass.

Hetland, L., Winner, E., Veenema, S., & Sheridan, K. (2007). *Studio thinking: The real benefits of visual arts education.* New York: Teachers College Press.

Hughes, L. (1994). Harlem[2]. In L. Hughes, *The collected poems of Langston Hughes* (p. 426). New York: Knopf.

Hutchins, E. H. (2008). Why make books? From Classroom connections. Book arts in the classroom. One artist. Many books. Retrieved August 11, 2008, from http://www.artistbooks.com/bookarts.shtml.

Neruda, P. (1997). Ode to the watermelon. In *Full woman, fleshy apple, hot moon. Selected poems of Pablo Neruda* (S. Mitchell, Trans., pp. 199–203). New York: Harper Perennial.

Preminger, A. (1965). *Princeton encyclopedia of poetry and poetics. Enlarged edition.* Princeton, NJ: Princeton University Press.

Rinaldi, C. (2001). Documentation and assessment: What is the relationship? In Project Zero/Reggio Children, *Making learning visible: Children as individual and group learners* (p. 79). Reggio Emilia, Italy: Reggio Children.

CHAPTER 11

Learning and Teaching Dance in the Elementary Classroom

Patty Yancey

Dancing Moons
I felt like I was on a moon of wonders.
The boys dancing dogs,
The girls dancing cats.
I felt like I was dancing on Fire.
I felt an angel when I was twirling.
I also felt like an angel when I was twirling.
I felt like I was flying when I was doing the movements.

—Carmela, K–5 student

I'VE BEEN TAKING dance class since I was 6 years old and have taught dance and creative movement to children, teens, and adults since 1987. Participating in dance classes held in a wide variety of physical spaces—green rooms, school gyms, multipurpose rooms, barns, playgrounds, and classrooms—has deepened my appreciation for the way instruction is organized in the "dance studio." As in the visual arts studio, instruction in the dance studio is organized by employing variations on a few basic patterns: demonstration-lecture, students-at-work, critique, and transitions (Hetland, Winner, Veenema, & Sheridan, 2007). This structure works in partnership with the teacher to foster attitudinal and thinking dispositions in the student as a result of regular participation in classes. The dispositions instilled in students are defined as "a trio of qualities—skills, alertness to opportunities to use these skills, and the inclination to use them—that comprise high-quality thinking" (p. 1)

In this chapter I will focus on how instruction is organized in the dance studio and how the studio habits of mind (Hetland et al., 2007) are developed in this learning environment. I will describe a dance unit that I designed for first graders while working as an artist-in-schools at George Peabody Elementary in

San Francisco. The unit is strong on developing technique—strength, coordination, flexibility, focus, and mental agility—through improvising, memorizing, creating, and rehearsing a variety of dance combinations over the course of a semester or school year. It can easily be adapted for upper elementary grades by accelerating the pace of the lessons. The unit can also be integrated with history/social studies to explore folk/traditional dances or with science to deepen understanding of concepts such as the life cycle, gravity, and rotation.

The lessons discussed in this chapter are the unit's introductory lessons that cover the organization and protocols of the dance studio, methods for constructing and teaching simple dance combinations, and an example of a lesson that integrates science and dance. This series of lessons can form a foundation for teaching any K–5 dance or creative movement unit.

INTRODUCTION TO DANCE

I introduce students to the vocabulary of dance and to dance as an art form before "stepping foot" in the studio. Counting and clapping to a steady beat, commands and signals used throughout the dance unit (i.e., "Zero Position" and "Freeze"), and expectations for behavior—as performers and as audience members—are also introduced during this introductory lesson. Videos, a field trip to a dance concert, or inviting a local dancer to the classroom as a guest artist are marvelous ways to pique the interest of and connect the students to the discipline and the profession of dance.

INTRODUCTION TO THE STUDIO

The organization of the dance space—physical environment and learning culture—is the foundation of the unit and is based on the traditional way of organizing space for teaching and rehearsing modern dance, ballet, jazz, and other forms of dance all over the world. This structure not only supplies you with an effective management and transition tool, it also motivates students to take responsibility for setting up and focusing themselves after the introductory lessons. All subsequent lessons in the unit rely on the framework and protocol that this structure provides. Your strongest dancers or most confident movers are positioned on the outside rows and columns of your formation, and your struggling dancers are placed on the inside. This configuration provides timid movers with models to follow for the majority of class time, no matter which way they turn during the session. It also contributes to the learning culture of the dance studio by creating a climate of cooperation and safety (Hetland et al., 2007).

After the instructor identifies positions and arranges the students in dance studio formation, they face the instructor and assume Zero Position. When students are in Zero Position bodies are still, and feet are slightly apart and planted firmly on

Figure 11.1. Organization of the dance studio.

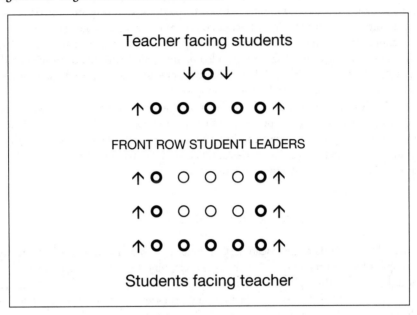

the ground. Hands are down at the sides, eyes are focused on the teacher, and there is absolutely no talking. The students are now ready to be positioned in the space to allow for freedom of movement:

- Ask them to slowly stretch out their arms to the sides. They should nudge themselves into position so that their outstretched fingertips barely touch the fingertips of their fellow students standing with outstretched arms in the rows to their right, left, or both.
- Arms down to sides.
- Turn 90 degrees to the right. Have all students stretch out their arms and repeat the exercise
- Repeat. Repeat. (Complete the circle.)
- Ask children to take a few moments to look at where they are in relation to the students around them. Direct them to independently move their bodies using axial movements, which means that students do not travel from their position in the dance formation. They can bend, contort, and sway their bodies; wave their arms; move their heads; lift and stretch their legs; bend their knees; and so forth. They should move in eight counts or beats, without traveling from the spot where they are standing. Count out loud for the students: "1–2–3–4–5–6–7–8."

- Ask children to assume Zero Position on the count of 8.
- Children repeat axial movement for 8 counts and assume Zero Position on the count of 8.
- Inform students again that it is their responsibility to remember their placement and to position themselves—and to help their classmates if they forget—the next time that dance class is held. After one or two lessons, students will be able to take responsibility for spacing themselves with minimal to no assistance.

After establishing positions and checking for understanding of commands, students are taught a combination that will be used throughout the unit as the warm up and closing ritual (cool-down) for each class. The combination should consist of 8 to 16 counts of upper-body stretches, spinal twists, forward bends, or shoulder rolls that flow together to create a smooth, continuous movement phrase that can be repeated indefinitely to create a composition.

The combination can be accompanied with music, a single percussion instrument, clapping, or finger-snapping to keep students in sync. The objectives of the warm-up/cool-down are to develop flexibility, balance, and control and to focus the mind and body. Transitioning from one movement to another within the warm-up must be simple enough so that the whole piece can be easily memorized and internalized. Restricting movement to the axial renders the warm-up/cool-down more versatile, allowing it to be practiced in tight spaces and outside on uneven terrain.

The following is an example of a 16-count warm-up/cool-down combination that can be accompanied by a slow, meditative piece of music or jazzed up with a lively, up-tempo number. Begin counting in 8s, out loud, to the beat, while students are standing in Zero Position awaiting the signal to begin moving. You can accompany the counting with a percussion instrument (e.g., hand drum or claves) or by clapping or snapping fingers. From Zero Position, students begin rolling down on the count of 1:

1—2—3—4	Roll down to touch toes. (Begin in Zero Position. Head rolls forward, leading upper body down toward the floor, legs straight. Fingers touch toes on count of 4.)
5—6	Hinge upper body up to flat back
7—8	Hinge to standing
1—2	Twist upper body to right
3—4	Twist upper body to left
5	Return to Zero Position—eyes open
6	Shut eyes TIGHT! Body still (Zero Position)
7	Eyes open WIDE! Body still (Zero Position)
8	Eyes normal. Body still (Zero Position)

Repeat. Repeat. Repeat.
Vary music.
Increase tempo.

The best way to approach a dance combination like this is to break it down into easily learned phrases. For a combination like the preceding 8-count warm-up, divide the 8 counts into two 4-count phrases and teach the phrases separately and sequentially:

1. Begin counting in 8s, out loud, to the beat, while students are standing in Zero Position observing: "1, 2, 3, 4, 5, 6, 7, 8; 1, 2, 3, 4, 5, 6, 7, 8; 1, 2," and so forth.
2. Model the whole combination a couple of times, while students continue to observe.
3. Next, begin to break it down. Model the first 4 counts of the combination a couple of times. Students are still in Zero Position, observing, awaiting the signal to begin moving.
4. Counting out loud, not dancing, give the students a couple of sets of 8 to establish the pace and rhythm.
5. Signal the students to start following along with their bodies.
6. On a count of 1, from Zero Position, students begin rolling their heads down to the floor.

The teaching of the 8-count phrase is structured in the following way: (1) Teach the first 4 counts—students observe teacher first, then follow along and practice, and teacher critiques; (2) teach the second 4-count phrase—students observe teacher first, then follow along and practice, and teacher critiques; (3) add the second 4-count phrase to the first 4 counts—repeat protocol; (4) students practice the full 8-count phrase repeatedly and teacher critiques.

The teacher alternates between the roles of instructor, audience, and critic—demonstrating, modeling, stepping back, and observing—continually providing feedback and encouragement and notes for improvement. After mastering the warm-up(s) students are taught a simple 32–count combination that introduces locomotor movement to the vocabulary. The term *locomotor* means that the body travels or moves across the floor (i.e., walking, skipping, galloping, etc.). The following 32-count combination can be learned quickly, repeated indefinitely, and varied with choice of music and change in tempo. It gets the blood circulating and wakes up the brain. Students begin in Zero Position.

1. Walk forward for 8 counts.
2. Side to side for counts 8—4 to the right, then 4 to the left.
3. Walk backward for 8 counts.
4. Walk side to side for 8 counts—4 to the right, then 4 to the left.

Again, the 32-count combination can be broken into as many phrases as necessary to facilitate learning. The protocol of warming up, reviewing previously learned combinations, learning new material, adding new material to previously learned combinations, rehearsing combinations to improve timing and technique, and reflecting and cooling down is repeated throughout the unit. The internalization of this protocol by teacher and students facilitates transitions and allows more time during the lessons for students to actually dance.

INTEGRATING DANCE WITH OTHER SUBJECT AREAS

In subsequent lessons, the teacher and students can begin their exploration and integration of another subject area into dance/creative movement. The fundamental structure of each lesson remains consistent and the teacher continues to alternate in the roles of instructor, audience, and critic—demonstrating, modeling, stepping back, observing, and providing feedback and encouragement and notes for improvement. The warm-up/cool-down combination learned in the introductory lessons continues to open and end each lesson.

Immediately following the warm-up, students review combinations and movements from prior lessons. During the review, students ask questions, practice, and clear up any confusion they may have about counts and sequences of the previously learned material. The objective is to build students' confidence to perform a variety of combinations as a group, on their own, without being led by the teacher. The review also focuses students and thoroughly warms up the body in preparation for learning new material.

Integrating Science and Dance

In an integrated science/arts lesson that I cotaught for kindergarteners and first graders, students began their investigation of how plants grow by planting seeds in containers, observing them daily, and recording their development in daily art journals.

After the warm-up and review, students were asked to sit on the floor, bend their knees, and wrap their arms around their legs. With their eyes closed and their bodies very still, I asked students to picture in their minds the seeds they had planted and had been monitoring daily. I then told the students a short yet richly descriptive story of a tiny seed that develops into a mature plant. In the second telling of the story, with the students' eyes still closed, I coached them to slowly move their bodies to mimic the gradual growth and development of their seedling. Students began moving one finger of one hand. This slight movement triggered movement in one arm. As the arm started to rise overhead, the fingers of the other hand started to flex. Then the bodies uncurled as if stretching after a long nap. As the fingers and arms stretched overhead, the students slowly rose to a standing position. I circled the room, offering feedback and direction, and continued talking students through the exercise until they were standing with arms stretched overhead, fingers extended. At that point, I directed the students: "Freeze!" I then told them to hold their poses for eight counts after they opened their eyes so they could see the variety of poses around them.

After my students resumed their seats on the floor, I led a discussion of their individual movement decisions. After this discussion, I assigned small groups of students different sets of environmental conditions. For example, one group portrayed seeds that were growing in an arid climate. Another group of seeds had been planted in rocky soil and another in rich, fertile soil, and so forth. I reminded students of their scientific observations and asked questions about how these conditions affected the growth of their seeds.

I clustered the students in their groups, and then talked them through the exercise, allowing them time to improvise and connect the quality of seed growth to their individual movements. After the lesson, when they were at their desks, students drew pictures of their poses in their journals.

In the next lesson of the series, I broke the students into the same groups and reviewed their particular soil and climate conditions. I then introduced an 8-count, steady beat and instructed them to grow from a seed to an adult plant in eight counts. On the count of 1, students were curled in tight balls on the floor. I counted to 8 in a slow and steady beat, accompanied by the claves. On the count of 8, with a loud strike of the claves, students "froze" in their plant pose. I then directed students to hold their poses for 8 additional counts. After these 16 counts, with students still frozen in their poses, they were directed to "melt" to the floor in 8 counts. The students "froze" in their positions on the floor on the 8th count, and then held the pose for 8 more counts. A quick discussion followed explicitly connecting the movement choices and qualities with the development of the seeds. The 32-count sequence was then repeated.

After students had the opportunity to practice repeatedly with the accompaniment of the teacher counting and striking the claves (or hand drum), I introduced an appropriate piece of music for the combination.

You may also want to integrate children's literature into the lesson to spark movement ideas. Rather than compose and tell your own story to the students of growing a seedling, do a read-aloud of *The Surprise Garden* (Hall & Halpern, 1999), *The Tiny Seed* (Carle, 2009), or *The Carrot Seed* (Krauss, 2004) and ask students to make movements inspired by the books.

Refining the Dance Combination and Deepening
Understanding of Science Content

Integrated lessons can be stretched over numerous, short, sequential 30- to 45-minute sessions. Students can learn to internalize the structure and strategies (i.e., studio formation, Zero Position, warm-up, review, cool-down) that facilitate transitions if the class location changes or if new students are added later in the semester.

A simple yet critical concept for students to grasp is that of "freezing." Students must freeze *immediately* on the teacher's command and remain frozen in that exact pose until they receive the signal to begin moving again (i.e., strike of the drum or claves). They learn that the contrast of moving versus not moving greatly affects the rhythm and energy of choreographed movement and the overall quality of the dance.

Additions of a read-aloud of a metaphor-rich story or a lesson on writing odes or acrostic poems (such as those described in Chapter 10) can further student understanding of the life cycle, as well as provide more opportunities for broadening students' vocabulary. During dance class, this vocabulary is used by the teacher to assist students in connecting the concepts of growth and development to how their own bodies feel and move.

The 32-count dance combination can be extended into a longer dance number with a few simple additions. For example:

- Have only one "group of seeds" grow at a time. Other groups stay frozen in tight balls on the floor until it is their time to grow. Repeat.
- After 24 counts, when students are standing "frozen" with arms overhead, direct them to wave and move in place for 16 counts, as if a strong wind is blowing. At the end of the 16 counts, students "freeze" for 8 counts, then melt down to the floor for 8 counts. Repeat.
- Add locomotor movement and allow students to travel around the dance floor in between the original 32-count sequence. Employ a locomotor phrase learned in Lesson 2 so that, with minimal additional practice, all students can move in unison.

The internalization by students of the structure and the strategies (i.e., studio formation, Zero Position, warm-up, review, cool-down) alleviates confusion or lost time if the class location changes or if new students are added later in the semester.

CLASSROOM AS DANCE STUDIO

The organization of the space in the dance studio formation "is a powerful factor in helping to accomplish instructional goals" (Hetland et al., 2007, pp. 15–16). It assumes the role of teacher's assistant in that it shapes "informal and sometimes more formal ways that students interact with one another and with teachers to create a social climate that nurtures learning" (p. 16). Being explicit with students about how their dance classes are organized and connecting it to the larger domain of the arts helps students link "what they do as students" to what professional dancers "do, have done, and are doing" (p. 7). It is important for the classroom teacher to make these sorts of connections visible to students so that the teaching and learning that go on in school are explicit to students and related to the real world.

The organization of time follows the "punctuated shape" that Hetland et al. (2007) identify as one of two basic ways of shaping class time. The punctuated shape sequence "employs shorter structures layered more frequently and at shorter intervals within a single class" (p. 30). In a dance class, multiple sets of demonstrations, students at work, critiques, transitions, and repetition play a major role in the teaching and learning and allow the teacher to refocus students on the habits of mind that he or she wants students to learn. New material is introduced incrementally, rather than as one demonstration-lecture delivered at the beginning of the class.

As the unit progresses, time spent transitioning between activities within a dance lesson, as well as transitioning from another subject to a dance lesson, is minimized. The *Studio Thinking* researchers recognize the critical importance of transitions and include it as a studio structure. They argue that "when poorly executed, transitions eat up valuable learning time, and when well-run, they may also provide a few more moments for focused, one-on-one interactions between teacher and students" (Hetland et al., 2007, p. 4). The teacher is able to focus on observing the students and dynamically assessing them on their ability to focus, remain alert, follow directions, stretch, and explore.

The unit effectively meets the California First Grade Content Standards for Dance in Artistic Perception, Creative Expression, Historical and Cultural Content, Aesthetic Valuing, and Connections, Relationships, and Applications. Hetland et al. clarify the relationship between the studio habits of mind and the content standards by noting that state and national standards specify particular levels and types of student achievement, and the "Studio Habits of Mind identify more general cognitive and attitudinal dispositions that allow students to meet these standards" (2007, p. 7).

CONCLUSION

I felt like a spy when we were doing the cross leg walk. I felt like a twirling pinwheel. I pretended to be as frozen as an ice cube. I could see the sunrise in the stretches. I could see the musicians in front of me. I turned into a springboard when we were doing the bounces. Thank you.

—Amiri, a student dance leader

In dance, the primary tool is the body. When students participate in ongoing, structured dance classes, they experience how rigorous practice affects the body—improving technique, strength, and stamina. Students learn the range of ways they can move, skillfully and mindfully, and they develop a sense of what they can and cannot do with their bodies. They also become more adept at making the right choices for the dances they are creating and performing.

In addition to improving coordination and balance, outcomes of a well-planned unit include students' learning how to organize and focus themselves for dance class—physically and mentally, individually and as a group—and internalizing the dispositions of working in a studio setting. Behaviors and habits of mind specific to working in the dance studio include occupying and working within one's space and not intruding into others', carefully observing the teacher's modeling of movements and remaining alert and open for instruction over an extended period of time, listening for verbal instructions and cues and translating them kinesthetically, being aware of dancers in motion around you, and partnering and collaborating with other dancers in the space. The integration of another subject, such as science or language arts, can provide new avenues for learning and furthering understanding of concepts, principles, and vocabulary by allowing the physical body to inform the intellectual.

The *Studio Thinking* framework has provided me with some valuable tools for making learning and teaching in the dance studio more accessible to practicing teachers, as well as the student teachers with whom I presently work. The *Studio* framework has also renewed my curiosity about whether the dispositions inculcated in students transfer to other subject areas. Although this question is still open to debate among researchers, my own experiences as a student and a teacher of dance offer me enough anecdotal data to continue to champion the inclusion of creative movement in the elementary classroom. With appropriate preservice and in-service professional development, even the most dance-challenged, multiple-subject classroom teacher can organize and facilitate a creative and well-structured learning experience in dance. If you feel this is a stretch for you, invite a dancer as a guest artist to your classroom for a series of lessons. Maximize the opportunity and participate as an arts learner along with your students.

REFERENCES

Carle, E. (2009). *The tiny seed*. New York: Little Simon.

Hall, Z., & Halpern, S. (1999). *The surprise garden*. New York: Blue Sky Press.

Hetland, L., Winner, E., Veenema, S., & Sheridan, K. M. (2007). *Studio thinking: The real benefits of visual arts education*. New York: Teachers College Press.

Krauss, R. (2004). *The carrot seed*. New York: HarperCollins.

CHAPTER 12

Working with K–12 Students

Teaching Artists' Perspectives

Ann Wettrich

OVER 25 years ago, my 2-year-old daughter would make drawings with distinct marks, illegible to me at first sight. However, as she named her drawings things like "streets and roads and sky," or "a 10-eyed face with grass," a picture of her thinking emerged. I saw that she was using words and lines to envision and shape her world, map and share her insights, make some sense of things, and connect with the world around her. She entered public school excited about learning, but that excitement seemed to diminish over the school year. Her drawings changed from wild, exploratory, and abstract narratives to stereotypical representations: the house in the middle of the page next to a tree, the family holding hands in front, the sun in the corner beaming down. I started to worry that her imagination was being tamped down and institutionalized. Because of funding cutbacks, there were no art teachers in the school. Teachers with little or no training in the arts were hard pressed to include the arts in the curriculum.

Fortunately, teaching artist and poet Gail Newman was working at the school through the California Poets in the Schools Program. In weekly poetry workshops, children were writing poems unique to each being and full of imaginative imagery, for example, "I am a penguin flying like an astronaut . . . my love is a compass without North . . ." When I asked my daughter how the drawing of a house and family would change if she thought of it as a poem, she transformed the landscape. The family members, formerly static, with two feet firmly planted on the ground, were now airborne and flying, and the trees now bowing from weather and wind. With permission and encouragement to use her imagination, the center of gravity shifted in her drawing, bringing the imagery to life and unleashing new possibilities.

Inspired by my daughter's ability to transfer what she was learning in poetry into another representational form, I began a visual arts collaboration with the poet. Through this experience, I came to understand how the arts can leverage learning and build school communities by forging connections across grade levels, cultures, classrooms, homes, and schools. As I saw the potential of the arts to revitalize the spirit and widen the enterprise of public education, I came to value the role of the teaching artist in achieving this vision.

Taking off from my own experience as a teaching artist and drawing on the voices of other teaching artists, this chapter will look at the role of teaching artists. Six teaching artists working in underresourced K–12 urban public schools share their ideas about and experiences of how they see the arts influencing teaching and learning and give their advice about how teachers can find teaching artists, build successful partnerships, and face challenges that can occur when artists and classroom teachers work together. They offer a vision for the future, and while each teaching artist's experiences and views are individually distinct and unique, they collectively affirm and reinforce a set of ideas, beliefs, and practices that speak to the power and possibilities of arts learning.

The following teaching artists contributed their perspectives for this chapter:

- Cathleen Micheaels (the author of Chapter 10) is a poet and book artist who enjoys interdisciplinary collaboration. She has 25 years of experience working with K–12 students and special populations, including at-risk and youth status offenders. Cathleen also provides professional development classes for preservice and classroom teachers.
- Sheila Balter is a theater artist and multilingual teacher of drama, creative movement, and music. She has taught K–12 students and teachers in public and private school and community contexts for 15 years and has especially enjoyed collaborating with dual-immersion language arts teachers. She has worked for many Bay Area nonprofit art education organizations and schools and has taught elementary school students at the French American School in San Francisco.
- Rebecca Shultz is a theater and visual artist who has been teaching theater for 8 years in the Bay Area. She has worked within school- and community-based programs, teaching students from preschool to adults. She has also worked with special populations, including disabled, incarcerated, and at-risk youth. She has worked as the art education program director for Community Works West.
- Elana Lagerquist is a theater artist and former elementary school teacher who has been working as a teaching artist for the past 7 years. She has worked in urban public and private schools, teaching theater and collaborating with teachers in art integration. She is a cofounder and codirector of StageWrite, a nonprofit art education organization that partners teaching artists with public schools.
- Ariel Roman is a visual artist with 4 years of teaching experience, with mostly urban high school students. She worked with the California College of the Arts' Center for Art and Public Life at the East Oakland School

of the Arts, teaching art and collaborating with a social studies teacher to integrate art into instruction.

- Gary Draper is a theater artist who has worked with Performing Arts Workshops (PAW) in a variety of capacities for 25 years, where he has taught drama and creative movement to K–12 public and private school students and their teachers throughout the Bay Area. As a PAW master teacher, Gary also coaches teaching artists.

My goal in this chapter is to inspire dialogue and creative collaborations among teachers and teaching artists that can lead to rich and enduring learning experiences, as both parties understand how to utilize and tap into each other's expertise. In the hands of skilled teachers and teaching artists, the arts can widen learning landscapes and help to connect ideas within and across subject areas.

WHO IS A TEACHING ARTIST?

We used to refer to artists working in the schools as *artists in residence*. Today we acknowledge the teaching role of artists and more commonly use the term *teaching artist* to refer to all kinds of artists who engage with schools and after-school and community programs. Over the past decade, the profession of teaching artist is coming to be named and recognized as teaching artists are forming associations and guilds to advance their work. The Association of Teaching Artists defines teaching artists as the following:

> A professional visual, performing, or literary artist who works in schools and in the community. The teaching artist may perform for the students and teachers, work in long-term or short-term residencies in classrooms or in a community setting, or lead in program development through involvement in curricular planning and residencies with school partners. The teaching artist is an educator who integrates the creative process into the classroom and the community. (Association of Teaching Artists, 2007)

Teaching artists first came into being to fill in the gaps as art education was dropped from the curriculum in response to "back-to-basics" educational thinking and as districts throughout the country cut budgets for full-time art teachers. Today, teaching artists collaborate with educators to integrate the arts into teaching and learning to achieve broad academic, developmental, and social educational goals called "arts learning." Teaching artists and the nonprofit art education sector also play a huge advocacy and fund-raising role to support the arts in schools. College course work and professional development programs are helping artists gain the knowledge and skills needed to better understand how to collaborate with educators to leverage learning in and through the arts.

HOW DO THE ARTS INFLUENCE TEACHING PRACTICE?

Scholar, writer, and art educator Sally Gradle (2007) theorizes that many of the qualities developed through artistic practice are important in the craft of teaching, including the ability to remain flexible, curious, willing to revise, take risks, and suspend closure in one's thinking of an idea. To get a clearer sense of the qualities to which Gradle refers, I asked teaching artists how their artistic practice influenced their teaching. All saw an integral relationship between art practice and teaching practice. Theater artists referred to teaching as a "performative act" and regularly used drama techniques—humor, timing, and improvisation—to engage students in learning. Visual artists described how dispositions intrinsic to the arts, like observation, reflection, and dialogue, are helpful in refining their practice and development as educators.

Further elaborating on art practice in the classroom, the teaching artists talked about how setting up a studio atmosphere in the classroom can transform the environment to motivate and draw students into learning. The classroom can become a safe, creative space, encouraging students to take risks, open up to possibilities, and stretch beyond the text. The classroom can become a multisensory lab where students can let go of stress, breathe, explore new ideas, and tap into their intuition and imagination.

Actor and director Sheila Balter describes how she utilizes theater games and warm-up processes to get to know her students. She takes the inspiration and the lead for her teaching from her students' "inner spark, their open, spontaneous, and organic manner of thinking." She is then able to tap their natural tendencies, curiosities, and interests to foster exploration and provide the tools, discipline, structure, and guidance to further develop and build on their thinking.

Poet and book artist Cathleen Micheaels describes the studio classroom as a place where students are challenged to discover and articulate who they are within the process of making and reflection, using their hands and minds to think and reflect. She stresses the investment of time needed to advance understanding and the emotional dimension of learning. As an artist, she has learned to be comfortable with struggle and the time it takes to investigate and work through ideas. In her teaching, she fosters patience and provides time for exploration, struggle, and making mistakes. She reiterates, "Doing something well doesn't happen automatically; mistakes lead to discovery and deep learning."

Clearly, art and teaching keep good company and occupy common ground. Intuitive, performative, interactive, improvisational, and fluid approaches are important to both art and teaching practice. Creative skills, along with organization, discipline, attentiveness, observation, reflection, revision, patience with problem solving, and the cultivation of persistence are necessary for teachers and artists. The integration of art and teaching practice offers valuable opportunities for professional exchange and growth among teaching artists and educators.

Teaching artists are aware of the constraints teachers face in establishing ideal conditions for learning. Working as allies with teachers, teaching artists believe that they can offer a set of new eyes, ears, and experiences to help address educational goals from a fresh perspective. Their hope is to bring an approach to teaching and learning that relieves restrictive testing regimens while opening opportunities for meaningful assessment and deep reflection, allowing for discovery and self-motivated learning through personal engagement and connection.

HOW DO THE ARTS INFLUENCE LEARNING?

Perhaps you have heard the claims from art education advocates that students involved in the arts do better in school and on their SATs than those who are not involved in the arts. We must ask ourselves if this is really true. If so, why? And is this a good enough reason to include the arts in the curricula?

The teaching artists had much to say about how the arts influence learning. Cathleen believes the process of inquiry inherent in the arts allows students to find a personal and "metaphorical truth" rather than literal or scientific proof. She explains how the arts help student to "work away from the known to the unknown." Students don't know where they're headed and there is no hidden answer the teacher holds. "The goal is discovery." Gary sees the focus and concentration that the arts require and help to build. Rebecca describes how the arts "tap multiple intelligences" and connect learning across disciplinary and other divides, playing to students' strengths. Elana points to the value of mistakes in the arts. Errors can propel learning, and exploration in the arts makes tangible the generativity of mistakes in sorting out, working through, talking about, and reflecting on problems that then lead to new questions, possibilities, and discoveries.

Sheila told a story of transformed expectation. By mistake, she gave a large part in a play to a student who she didn't know was diagnosed as "learning disabled." Had she known, she would not have given the student a major role, fearing that she'd be setting her up for embarrassment and failure. All were surprised, as the student seized this opportunity to show she was capable. She learned all her lines, better than most other students, and gave an amazing performance. Sheila commented on how art teaches students to trust their inner voice and being, that "art is a friend," not telling them to do anything specific, but functions as "a guide," encouraging explorations of the possibilities of the imagination in relationship to living. "It helps students to think outside the box and fosters proclivity in movement and free expression."

Teaching artists talk about the arts as a "window" into understanding humanity and as an essential way of coming to know, understand, and shape the world. They emphasize the value of the arts in seeing beyond our own horizon, history, culture, and environment while helping to affirm and develop our own unique voice and identity. They help students develop a sense of agency, magic, freedom, and delight. Exploding narrow definitions and expanding opportunities for success within and beyond formal schooling, the arts open access to multiple forms of expression and diverse avenues of inquiry that enable us to celebrate, critique, reimagine, and transform our world.

ARTS LEARNING PARTNERSHIPS—SUCCESS STORIES AND LESSONS LEARNED

On the ground, working within current time constraints and competing educational priorities, many teachers see art integration as a way to begin providing students with the benefit of arts learning. Additionally, they see partnerships with teaching artists as a way to garner badly needed expertise in the arts in order to plan and implement successful arts-integrated lessons. Let's take a look at what successful partnerships between teaching artists and teachers are yielding from teacher artists' perspectives.

Sheila related a story about a partnership with an elementary teacher at a Spanish bilingual school in San Francisco. She and a teacher with little knowledge or experience in the arts established a deep rapport and made the time to work together to create a series of integrated units involving creative movement, music, and language arts. The students choreographed a dance and composed and performed songs in Spanish. The teacher rehearsed with the students in between sessions with the teaching artist and through this experience began to understand and value how the arts leveraged learning as she saw the engagement of her students. She noticed that when they weren't performing they were observing and fully present with attentive minds. The following year, after the partnership ended, this teacher capitalized on what she learned, confidently refining and building on the art-integrated lessons and teaching practices.

Elana knows that the partnership is working when both she and the teacher want to do more. They get energized through the process of organic brainstorming where they keep getting ideas from each other. She finds teachers used to working alone in the classroom especially value this. Productive collaboration is visible, as creative synergy builds and the teacher and teaching artist want to do more than what is expected.

IDENTIFYING CHALLENGES AND OPPORTUNITIES

It goes without saying that there are as many challenges as opportunities within arts learning partnerships. It is wise to understand and be prepared to address the challenges in order to reap the richest rewards.

According to teaching artists, the most frequent challenge to partnerships is perceived lack of time, resources, and capacity. In these cases, the arts can be just another thing added into an already densely loaded school day, or a luxury teachers cannot afford in schools that are under pressure to meet testing benchmarks for "adequate yearly progress." Accomplishing deep learning in and through the arts, as many of the teaching artists have noted, requires a serious commitment and investment of time, not just hit-and-miss, fill-in-the-gap programs.

Foremost among the common challenges reiterated by teaching artists are misconceptions about the arts. Because the value of arts learning is not fully understood, schools with limited resources often emphasize product over process. This means less time on the creative process, where much of the learning takes place. Pressure to produce an exhibition or performance within a constrained time frame puts an unbalanced emphasis on the final product. In these situations, genuine collaboration is not possible, and the quality of teaching and learning suffers.

Another important concern on the part of artists is that they are not seen as experienced professionals and are undervalued by schools in terms of pay, quality of materials provided, and respect for their time. Several teaching artists related experiences where schools called them at the last minute to cancel a class or they arrived at school to find out that an assembly had preempted their class with no apologies offered. Others talked about clashing approaches to teaching, saying that nonarts teachers sometimes have very concrete plans and objectives set in stone and find it difficult to be flexible. In teaching and integrating the arts, flexibility is a must.

When working well, partnerships make rich, enhanced learning possible and provide the means for engaging and reaching students who have turned away from learning in other modes. The arts hold the promise of enlarging the scope of education, bringing joy into teaching and learning. As the teaching artists' stories reveal, the arts build learning communities that enable us to voice our experience, bridge human divides, construct meaning, and build understanding within and across subject areas. For this ideal vision to be realized, providing all students with equitable access to the advantages of high-quality arts learning, much work needs to be done in advancing capacity, knowledge, and skills among teaching artists and teachers, as well as building an infrastructure to support the work.

LEVERAGING RESOURCES AND BUILDING CAPACITY

What do successful art-integration partnerships entail? What do teachers need to know to incorporate the arts into their classrooms; what role do teaching artists play? What are some successful practices? What resources are available to teachers? Much has been written on this topic, but here we will take a look at this from the teaching artist's perspective. First we will explore capacity-building strategies for nonarts teachers. How do nonarts teachers bring arts learning opportunities to their students? Not surprisingly, the top answer to this question is *through partnerships with teaching artists*. Drilling down a bit, beyond contracting teaching artists to work with students in the classroom, what are the other ways teachers can strengthen their capacity to bring arts learning experiences to their students? Teaching artists say:

- Take time to talk with teaching artists and ask for recommendations on art education readings, exercises, and tools specific to classroom needs and goals.
- Observe teaching artists working directly with students.
- Seek professional development or coaching to expand knowledge and skills in a variety of art forms and media.
- Consider becoming a student teacher to an artist as a way to learn.
- Develop a collegial learning exchange with other teachers and teaching artists to share ideas and problem-solve.

When asked what she thinks is most important for teachers to understand in guiding arts learning experiences for their students, Sheila replied that teachers should know that "the results may not be immediate or perfect; the process is the learning experience, it's not about product; and you can do it!" She wants teachers to see that the artist is not a threat, but brings a different way of working and can provide additional ways of achieving the educational goals that the teacher holds for the students. Elana replied that teachers should understand how to change the configuration of a classroom into an artistic environment and to be comfortable with managing "structured chaos."

Cathleen thinks it is important for teachers to make art so that they can understand the problems and challenges that students encounter and can help to guide their learning. Experiences making art can help teachers understand what students are feeling and learn how to troubleshoot. Gary, too, emphasizes that when an artist comes into the classroom to work with students, he would like teachers to understand the importance of their own active engagement in the project. Ariel wants teachers to know that in teaching visual art "they don't have to be able to draw, that art is more than painting and drawing and Picasso."

PARTNERSHIP KNOW-HOW

Given that partnerships are a key strategy in advancing and realizing the advantages of arts learning, teaching artists offer their ideas about how to make such partnerships successful. They highlight the importance of planning and evaluation time, collaboration, space, and classroom management.

For partnerships to succeed, a commitment to planning and evaluation is essential. Before beginning the partnership project, "get on the same page." Get to know each other, develop a work plan and schedule, and clarify goals, expectations, and communication mechanisms. It is also important to provide for ongoing planning and evaluation time throughout the partnership in order to debrief and reflect on what is working and what isn't and to make responsive adjustments.

Build trust, communicate regularly, and be open to each other's ideas. Respect and utilize the expertise and perspectives of all participants in the partnership. You should expect to participate with the teaching artist in the classroom either as coteacher, assistant, participant, or observer. Identify how you can continue to integrate the arts and develop arts learning when the teaching artist is not there.

Be open to rearranging the room and letting it get messy during partnership activities. Be sure to clarify management issues and routines. Make explicit agreements about the roles and responsibilities of teacher and teaching artist in relation to discipline.

FINDING A TEACHING ARTIST PARTNER: QUALITIES TO LOOK FOR

Teaching artists recommend doing research and seeking help and advice from colleagues and teachers at other schools with arts partnerships. Good resources include district visual and performing arts offices, local art commissions, county offices of education, art education service organizations, art colleges, university art departments, museums, and community cultural organizations. Information can also be gathered from state and national art education service organizations. Teachers are encouraged to look for art education organizations with a philosophy and set of goals that match theirs and the school's and that provide professional development for the teaching artists they employ.

It is important to interview and observe teaching artists to get to know them personally and professionally. This way you and your school will be in a better position to assess whether the teaching artist is a good fit. One teaching artist passed on questions to ask at an interview:

- Why is teaching important to you?
- What motivates you?
- What is your art education philosophy?

Together the teaching artists point to three areas—knowledge, skills, and dispositions—you should investigate when interviewing teaching artists. In terms of knowledge, look for deep understanding of subject matter content and skills and how arts can leverage learning across disciplines. Teaching artists should also be knowledgeable about school culture and environment, as well as teaching and learning theories and practices, including multicultural and antiracist education. As far as skills, teaching artists should be able to collaborate. They should be organized and understand how to structure learning experiences. They should be flexible and remain open to change, able to listen, skilled at aligning arts with educational goals, and culturally competent and able to engage diverse learners. Regarding personal attributes and dispositions, teaching artists recommend that teachers look for partners who are compatible, responsible, respectful of others, fun loving, and curious. They should value diversity; bring new perspective and expertise; and be active in their own artistic pursuits, research, and development.

Remember that teaching artists most often work as independent contractors and don't receive health insurance and employment benefits. When negotiating rates of pay, take into account both level of education and experience and remember that teaching artists are skilled professionals. Mindful teachers and teaching artist allies are aware of the shared and distinct knowledge and skills they bring to the classroom and appreciate the collegial relationship and professional growth they gain from working together to provide engaging and meaningful learning opportunities for students.

ENVISIONING THE FUTURE

If we are to develop a vision for education that embeds the arts in teaching and learning, what will it look like? What is needed to get there? Where do teaching artists fit into this picture? This is the concluding set of questions I put to the teaching artists.

Teaching artists responded by emphasizing a need to transform education into a system that is about teaching to the whole child, where knowing, understanding, and respect for all children and their creative intelligences, cultures, and learning styles are valued. They speak about a necessary paradigm shift in value systems away from industrial and behaviorist models for education toward a more progressive, nonprescriptive, creative, inquiry-based pedagogy, attendant to the highest standards while being responsive to the interests and lives of students. Teaching artists believe that the arts can be a resource in shaping and realizing a broader vision for education. They would like to see all the arts included in the curriculum, with professional teaching artists working in long-term partnerships with schools. They envision systemic change with the arts linked to learning across subject areas and utilized as a means to develop and activate a sense of connection and community at the schools, involving families, teachers, administrators, and staff.

How do we make this vision of education come alive? Teaching artists suggest developing advocacy and networking alliances, garnering more resources to create opportunities, providing professional development to strengthen teaching artist–teacher partnerships, raising public awareness about the value of art in learning, and creating a diversity of models with more experimenting and research to figure out what works and putting these ideas into practice. One artist identified a need to shift the values of the art world so that artists would begin to better understand their important relationship to the community and to see the important role they can play in public education. The evolving role for teaching artists within this vision requires acknowledging the value of their work and establishing their place within the larger educational system. Professionalizing their role within the education system means providing living wages, benefits, and professional development opportunities and developing standards of practice. The idea is for arts to be woven into the culture of teaching and learning, and for teaching artists to build enduring collegial relationships with teachers—to become essential threads in the fabric of schools.

REFERENCES

Association of Teaching Artists. (2007). *What is a teaching artist?* Retrieved December 31, 2007, from http://www.teachingartists.com/whatisaTA.htm

Gradle, S. (2007). Random weave: Developing dispositions to teach art. *Art Education Journal, 60*(4), 6–11.

Afterword

Lois Hetland

READING THIS manuscript at the height of a rainy midsummer, I already find myself eager for fall: itchy, excited, ready to get back to work. The wellspring of experience depicted by this collection of wise artist educators is an antidote to any external dreariness, and it calls us back to the important work in arts education that we do together across the country and the world.

As I read the voices of teaching artists, artist-teachers, arts administrators, and professors of arts and general education in Northern California, my own career history spins in memory. Mine has been a series of transitions—from teacher to researcher, and now to college professor—and that's required frequent adjustments to my vision. For almost 20 years in Pre-K–7 classrooms, I lived in immediacy—from moment to moment, children did or didn't engage, thrive, learn—and I responded as best I could. As a researcher, though, I've learned to be patient about seeing effects and to live more indirectly and vicariously. Once we have findings, it's time to put them out into the world. And then, you wait. Are there any signs that the research completed offers support to teachers in managing the dilemmas they face in addressing children's needs? Usually, it is hard to know: a review here, a comment there, the thanks from someone after a talk.

But rarely have I seen so vividly as in this book the interactions between research endeavors and the ongoing efforts of teachers as they strive to do more for their students. It's especially heartening to see the uses these authors are making of what my colleagues at Project Zero and I have created. There are so many examples in this remarkable work of how teachers are *thinking with* the Studio Thinking Framework (Hetland, Winner, Veenema, & Sheridan, 2007), thinking dispositions (Perkins, Jay, & Tishman, 1993; Tishman, Jay, & Perkins, 1993), the Teaching for Understanding Framework (Blythe and Researchers and Teachers, 1998; Wiske, 1998), the tenets of Making Learning Visible (Project Zero/Reggio Children, 2001), the ideas of multiple intelligences (Gardner, 1983), and entry points to learning experiences (Gardner, 1991, 1999). It's astonishing, like seeing flesh grow on bones.

If education is to rejuvenate, if new generations of teachers and artists are to learn from the past and come to children with fresh, heartfelt, effective strategies for teaching them to learn, then it's examples such as these that will teach them. I can hardly wait to offer these chapters to my own students at the Massachusetts College of Art and Design who are entering their own practice as art educators; they so desperately want and need such visions of what classrooms can be. I am grateful to the authors of this book, who labored to put their understanding into words for this text. As a reader and colleague, I thank you.

We need detailed images such as these of learning experiences, in which classrooms feed and enrich students' fascination and curiosity while giving them the tools to notice what makes sense, what doesn't, how to pursue finding out, how to represent and share that, and how to revel in the satisfaction of serious efforts brought to fruition. How far the images in this book are from the stark, rote, and ritual scenes I've heard described by teachers in the past decade. They've told me about hour after hour of deadly "drill and kill" preparation for the tests that haunt so many schools today. Recently, someone described to me "directed reading," in which the class reads along with their teacher word by word, from books with limited vocabularies; safe, inoffensive stories; and easy morals. Hearing about it chokes me, and I don't even have to sit through it. These are not the stories told in song that the ASCEND kindergartners used as their textbooks for learning to read, or the poems Cathleen Micheaels's students penned into their books. While such innovative practices apparently run against the current grain, they actually have a deep cultural legacy in American schools. An example from Bailey White's *Mama Makes Up Her Mind* (1993) shows what I mean. Ms. White used "maritime disasters" as a topic and sea shanties as texts to teach reading to her first graders: "So his messmates pulled him up, but on the deck he died," and "He sank into the Lowland, Lowland, low, he sank into the Lowland Sea" (p. 170). Such methods are as fresh today in Oakland's Fruitvale district and San Francisco's community arts learning venues as they were in White's south Georgia classroom or one-room schoolhouses like those my father attended in the Midwest.

As I soaked in the manuscript, themes began to emerge from the stunning images of planning, teaching, and learning that are portrayed in these chapters. I offer these themes and a few thoughts about each here, hoping that my synthesis will prompt readers' own quests to seek the deeper structures that connect the detailed, real-life examples illustrated in this book.

• *One step at a time*: Over and over, the artists and teacher authors show how they started small, used resources at hand, and built from what they knew, tweaking already good practice into better practice. Maybe we should bring that phrase into use: *better practices*. Nice ring. And truer to what really happens in teaching than *best practices*—good work always seems to grow organically from wherever it is at any moment, with teachers adjusting and accommodating from what is, to aspire continually toward what they want for students.

• *Emphasizing passion*: These authors went for what drew them. Often, they describe identifying something that they wanted, which frequently arose from images, experiences, and understandings developed in their own pasts. For students, too, the authors focus on engaging passion: Evan Hastings describes engaging students through their personal conflicts and losses; Cathleen Micheaels through the interactions between books, poetry, and fruits and vegetables; Dafney Dabach through evocative photographs; Arzu Mistry through the tribulations of a local creek; and so forth. Finding and holding on to passions motivates thoughtful action, inquiry, and persistence, for both teachers and students—engage! When passion is separated from the learning process, we risk making learning into a flattened routine without purpose and, ultimately, into an exercise no one can wait to finish, rather than the exciting discovery that clutches us and makes time dissolve—"flow," in Csikszentmihalyi's (1990) terms—when learning is pursued genuinely. It's that genuine pursuit that I feel throughout these chapters: These teachers and their students care about what's being undertaken, and that's what leads to persistence.

• *Holding the center iteratively*: These authors articulate core sets of ideas that they return to habitually; doing so keeps the focus of experiences on the learning they intend and makes that learning a shared purpose for everyone in the classroom. Some authors talk about that through elements of the Teaching for Understanding Framework, Understanding Goals or Throughlines, which are public, posted questions that focus on big ideas (Blythe and Researchers and Teachers, 1998; Wiske, 1998). It is that dynamic movement from actual experiences to larger ideas represented by the Throughline or Understanding Goal, over and over, that binds the practical actions of learning to what matters at a more universal scale.

• *Frameworks as support*: Notably, many authors specifically cite "thinking frames" (Perkins, 1986, 1987) developed by Project Zero, and the Studio Thinking Framework in particular. But often teachers combine Project Zero's frames with a range of other frameworks that they find useful in their own work. It is thrilling to see this! The complex reality of arts and arts-integrated classrooms needs a clear armature to hold it up, to keep it centered, to hear the main melody within the counterpoints of the moment-to-moment connections made by individuals and groups, and the authors often describe using thinking frames to hold to their own core intentions. Frameworks are lenses that can help people see more, and seeing more allows seeing more clearly what *is*. That reflective linking of perception and thought leads to better decisions and choices about how to use the precious and limited time available for learning experiences. Violet Juno, for example, shows how she blends two Project Zero frameworks, Teaching for Understanding and Making Learning Visible. Sarah Willner refers to Teaching for Understanding's "Understanding Goals" when she says, "Whenever you are publicly emceeing an event, point out the understanding goals for a project and honor the students for achieving these goals." In addition, she sees her work as a music educator more clearly by blending Gardiner's values of music, her school's "Six Ways to ASCEND," Expeditionary Learning, and the California Visual and Performing Arts standards with Studio Habits of Mind. Evan Hastings mixes theater of the oppressed, drama therapy, and elements of hip-hop culture into social healing through drama, and he analyzes the dispositions he intends students to learn with the Studio Habits. Patty Yancey uses Studio Habits as lenses for teaching dance.

Using multiple lenses to see their students' work—and their own—helps teachers view teaching and learning from several perspectives and understand its nuances and complexities. Synthesizing those perspectives provides a deeper appreciation of the entire enterprise. Such synthesis requires working back and forth repeatedly between single moments of learning to more general categories and back again iteratively. That is the dialogue, both internal and shared with other professionals, that teachers use to hone successful ways to better teach particular students and particular content. These authors show us many times how they engage in such a dynamic learning process by considering the daily events of teaching and learning through research-based frameworks. Back and forth. That tension between the grounded immediate and some general categories creates a valuable fuel for powering the engines of learning.

• *Reflective collaborations*: Too often, teachers work in isolation from adult colleagues. Ann Wettrich's chapter focuses on the advantages that ensue when artists and classroom teachers work together, and many of the other chapters also reveal how collectives of teachers can leverage each other's professional expertise. Such collaborations are demonstrated by a great deal of research as being critical to teachers being able to sustain and develop their capacities to nurture compelling learning environments over time (e.g., Newmann and Associates, 1996). I hope administrators will take serious note—bringing teachers together to learn from and with each other, whether observing each other teach, coteaching, co-planning, being critical friends in teacher action research or study groups, or working in vertical disciplinary teams across the age spans, is a "better practice" way to offer effective professional development. Why is it so rare?

• *Modeling collaboration*: There is a great divide in the field of education between communities of expert practice and educational research. Too often, the flow of wisdom about what should be taught and learned is severely restricted by these barriers: Artists talk only to artists, scholars talk among themselves, teachers are usually isolated even from each other, and families are left out entirely. *Artful Teaching* represents another way, in which the many groups concerned with rigorous learning for children and youth overlap and permeate one another. Artists, teachers, and parents/guardians work together; researchers learn from teachers and artists and families; and everyone offers back their perspectives. The professional learning cycles endlessly.

• *Solutions to practical problems*: How could one make an *aesthetic* exhibition of learning that communicates clearly, without too much or too little text, or without too many or no clear ideas? When students move beyond safety for themselves or each other during a learning experience, how can teachers respond without disrupting and, preferably, by enhancing, the creative flow of learning? Can we design classroom space to support inquiry, collaboration, and exploration in a variety of media? What does it look like when arts are integrated well with other arts and nonarts subjects? These chapters are replete with effective ways the authors have designed to deal with problems every teacher faces. It is an inspirational collection of evidence about the wisdom that resides in experienced educators.

• *Thought is front and center*: Arts are making and doing; but making and doing are acts of *mind*, and that is explicitly acknowledged by these artist-teacher-authors. The editors frame thinking as the task of teachers—rethinking their teaching by reflecting on what they do, what they want, and how to get it. Laurie Polster specifically names thinking as central to what art is. Louise Music places "thinking frames" (Perkins, 1986, 1987) at the heart of the Alliance for Arts Learning Leadership; they offer categories to think in and vocabulary for communicating that thinking. Classroom educators, too, emphasize thinking: Teachers describe asking students explicitly to think with the Studio Habits of Mind; Violet Juno mentions "thinking walls" (Hetland, Cajolet, & Music, 2009) that are set up for regular reflection sessions with classes; Debra Koppman describes how reflective thinking "helps students and teachers connect arts learning to writing." All this makes a potent statement about the arts' place at the core of learning. Art is thinking, and who wants to argue against thinking being at learning's center?

• *Contemporary arts are usually central*: This observation is tightly linked to thinking being at the fore of learning, and also linked to the importance of schools maintaining connections with practicing artists, whether state-licensed artist-teachers or teaching artists. Contemporary art and the artists who make it are founts of possibility, since in contemporary art, meaning is central, with craft in the art media taking a supporting role. Meaning in contemporary arts includes such ideas as social justice and equity; identity; cultural heritage; youth culture; globalization; and contemporary historical, scientific, narrative, and philosophical issues of all sorts. The media and methods used to represent those ideas are frequently developed by artists in response to their intentions. This is a critical feature of all the work described in these chapters—the authors describe leading with meaning and following with technique. Doing so gives a context for the skills students need to develop, and that context motivates both engagement and persistence. Sticking to that mantra in K–12 art education—lead with meaning, follow with technique—would make it easier for fellow teachers, parents, administrators, school boards, and members of the public who are not conversant in the nuances of art to see the many connections to general education. And that's important. For arts to be effective, everyone needs to see arts as central to a quality general education.

• *Arts support difference; difference as a resource*: "The arts are for everyone; they are part of our world, rather than just for the talented few," says Sarah Willner. Understanding arts in this way means that the arts can be a primary tool for differentiating instruction, and it shows throughout these chapters. Through arts, students reveal their identities, and astute teachers learn to listen and watch so that they can understand their students' growing edges and support them. But arts not only *allow* differentiated teaching, they also celebrate difference as a personal and cultural resource. These authors clearly recognize that each child is unique and that their unique qualities give teachers and other students opportunities to learn. It is through seeking balance around apparent opposites that labor bears fruit.

• *Families as resources for equitable learning*: Lynda Tredway and Rebecca Wheat describe how arts leaders focus on the necessity of involving families when developing arts programs, and many of the other authors describe ways in which they invite parents into educational discussions and practice, tapping them as resources from which teachers can learn. Parents know their children, their heritage and neighborhoods; are sometimes practitioners of various arts, including folk arts; and offer fresh eyes from their own experiences onto important processes, products, places, and power struggles. It is wonderful to have so many ideas offered in these chapters about how to make the most of the rich reservoir of wisdom and possibility offered by families—if we only ask.

• *Arts united with arts integration*: In efforts to protect the integrity of the arts as a genuine discipline worthy of study in its own right, arts educators have sometimes placed the teaching of arts in opposition to arts integration. This is a mistake. Alone, neither approach is enough, but using them together magnifies the effects of both. This book offers vivid examples of how educators of all stripes—art; nonart; school based; out of school; in all art forms; amateur or professional; from local, national, or global contexts—all interact to offer students a richer education. I urge the field to stop pitting these two approaches to arts learning against each other, since they are natural allies, not mutually exclusive alternatives. We need a pantheon of arts educators, all of whom contribute aspects of what art offers to those who use it to improve their lives.

I hope this brief reflection on some of the themes found in these chapters inspires readers to look back more closely across the book to find connections that inspire them, which I hope will lead to their own innovations. We all need to advance this work further, leading out from this center in whatever directions our interests take us. For myself, I'm reminded of my own passion for digging further into the connections between professional art practice and art teaching, an interest that grows from a comment by my colleague Steve Locke at the Massachusetts College of Art and Design. Steve saw the connection between his own painting practice and art education through the Studio Habits that strikes me as powerful, and I want to know more.

I'm also exploring assessing arts learning with the Studio Habits. I'm particularly drawn to a metaphor I've begun using recently to describe levels of learning with the states of matter: solid, liquid, and gas. Solid levels are rote and ritual with extrinsic motivations—too often, school subjects begin and end at this level; liquid levels show when students think with what they know, motivated intrinsically. At this level, categories are permeable and responsive to students' contexts and needs.

That's where we want K–12 students to be, and making art readily takes them there. Finally, the gaseous level represents expertise, in which membranes between categories are so permeable that they almost cease to exist and the gas escapes the container. Try testing those levels on a standardized paper-and-pencil test!

Students need the categories to begin to understand and take charge of their own developing expertise, and it seems to me that we profit by moving them into the "liquid" level of using ideas together very early—from the start. But I digress.

Let me conclude by reiterating that I find the result of these authors' efforts stunning. For me, the volume stands as a testament to what educators might offer to students and society if we can move beyond our insular walls and the hierarchies that they breed. Opening our visions wider and taking the time to reflect together certainly will not always be easy; in fact, it will often uncover treacherous tensions. But we cannot shy from these tensions. Embracing them seems the most direct path to innovations like those so beautifully revealed in these chapters. If we use them as opportunities, like artists use errors and Baily White (1993) used maritime disasters, the tensions and challenges can show us the way forward, toward a goal we all embrace: quality education for all children.

I can end only by saluting the authors once more and saying again, hurray! for the ongoing work in Northern California! Long may it wave!

REFERENCES

Blythe, T., and the Researchers and Teachers of the Teaching for Understanding Project. (1998). *The teaching for understanding guide.* San Francisco: Jossey-Bass.

Csikszentmihalyi, M. (1990). *Flow: The psychology of optimal experience.* New York: Harper & Row.

Gardner, H. (1983). *Frames of mind.* New York: Basic Books.

Gardner, H. (1991). *The unschooled mind: How children think and how schools should teach.* New York: Basic Books.

Gardner, H. (1999). *The disciplined mind: What all students should understand.* New York: Simon & Schuster.

Hetland, L., Cajolet, S., & Music, L. (2009). Documentation in the visual arts: Cross-pollinations of theory and practice. Submitted to *Theory into Practice.*

Hetland, L., Winner, E., Veenema, S., & Sheridan, K. (2007). *Studio thinking: The real benefits of visual arts education.* New York: Teachers College.

Newmann, F., and Associates. (1996). *Authentic achievement: Restructuring schools for intellectual quality.* San Francisco: Jossey-Bass.

Perkins, D. N. (1986). Thinking frames. *Educational Leadership, 43*(8), 4–10.

Perkins, D. N. (1987). Thinking frames: An integrative perspective on teaching cognitive skills. In J. B. Baron & R. J. Sternberg (Eds.), *Teaching thinking skills: Theory and practice* (pp. 41–61). New York: W. H. Freeman.

Perkins, D. N., Jay, E., & Tishman, S. (1993). Beyond abilities: A dispositional theory of thinking. *Merrill-Palmer Quarterly, 39*(1), 1–21.

Project Zero/Reggio Children. (2001). *Making learning visible: Children as individual and group learners.* Reggio Emilia, Italy: Reggio Children.

Tishman, S., Jay, E., & Perkins, D. N. (1993). Teaching thinking dispositions: From transmission to enculturation. *Theory into Practice, 32,* 147–153.

White, B. (1993). *Mama makes up her mind.* Reading, MA: Addison-Wesley.

Wiske, M. S. (Ed.). (1998). *Teaching for understanding: Linking research with practice.* San Francisco: Jossey-Bass.

About the Editors and Contributors

DAFNEY BLANCA DABACH, PhD, recently finished her doctorate in education at the University of California, Berkeley. Her research focused on how teachers adapted to their secondary English learner students. Also a photographer, she has exhibited her work in the United States and Mexico and is delighted to be involved in efforts to link arts integration with immigrant education.

DAVID M. DONAHUE, PhD, associate professor of education, Mills College, Oakland, California, works with teacher credential students preparing to teach art, English, and history in secondary schools and with graduate students investigating teaching and learning with a focus on equity in urban contexts. His research interests include teacher learning in general and learning from the arts and service learning specifically.

CYRUS E. DRIVER is deputy director of the Educational Opportunity program of the Ford Foundation. His portfolio has supported broad-based collaborative efforts to reform large urban school districts and state community college systems in the United States so that all their students, particularly those from historically marginalized groups, receive a high-quality education needed to participate fully in American society.

TODD ELKIN is a visual artist and arts educator. He currently teaches visual arts at the high school level and is a research assistant on the Harvard/Project Zero's Project Zero Schools Initiative. His current research involves examining what happens when students pay attention to their artistic process.

EVAN HASTINGS, MA, adjunct professor for creative arts in learning, Lesley University, Cambridge, Massachusetts, integrates Theatre of the Oppressed, Drama Therapy, and elements of the hip-hop culture into his approach to artistic social healing. He facilitates hip-hop theater classes in schools and correctional facilities and supports educators in strengthening arts integration through consulting and professional development.

LOIS HETLAND, EdD, is professor of art education at the Massachusetts College of Art and Design, and a research associate at Harvard/Project Zero. Trained in music and visual arts, she taught K–12 for 17 years, was founding chair of Project Zero's annual summer institute, and collaborates in research in Alameda County, California, funded by the U.S. Department of Education.

STEPHANIE VIOLET JUNO, MFA, is nationally known for her work as a performance artist, visiting professor, and master teaching artist. As a disabled person, she dedicates her work with students every day to the teachers and teaching artists who helped her find a way through the pain to engage deeply with the fascinating and challenging world we live in.

DEBRA KOPPMAN, DA (Doctor of Arts), has worked for the past 11 years as an artist-in-residence at Sequoia Elementary, a public K–5 school in Oakland, California. She has taught art practice and theory at universities in California, Mexico, and Peru. She has exhibited her work in sculpture, handmade paper, and book arts widely.

CATHLEEN MICHEAELS, arts education consultant, works with county offices of education, school districts, nonprofit organizations, and teacher education programs to bring the literary and visual arts into teaching and learning across school communities. For over a decade, Ms. Micheaels worked with Civicorps Schools in Oakland, California, most recently supporting the development of service learning and arts integration curriculum resources and teacher internship credentialing partnerships.

ARZU MISTRY, EdM, is a research associate with Project Vision, an education research collective at the Srishti College of Art Design and Technology in Bangalore, India. She is dedicated to the arts as a medium of personal empowerment, positive social change, and an essential part of teaching and learning.

LOUISE MUSIC is the director of the Alameda County Office of Education's Alliance for Arts Learning Leadership, a network of 18 school districts and community partners in Alameda County, California. Through comprehensive regional, state, and national partnerships, the work in Alameda County connects learning in and through the arts to a new vision for a rigorous, relevant, and responsive public education across the curriculum.

LAURIE POLSTER, MFA, is an interdisciplinary artist/vocalist/musician and arts educator who teaches and consults in public and private schools and nonprofit organizations in the San Francisco Bay Area. She has received numerous fellowships, awards, and artist residencies, and her work is exhibited nationally. As an educator and arts integration coach, she focuses on developing tangential awareness, making linkages across disciplines, and infusing education with creative processing that challenges and broadens understanding.

JENNIFER STUART, arts coordinator at San Francisco Friends School, San Francisco, teaches middle school art and works with the faculty at her school to integrate art into their general practice. She has also provided professional development to educators through organizations, including the Center for Art and Public Life at the California College of the Arts, the Bay Area Teachers Collaborative, the San Francisco Art Commission, and Harvard/Project Zero. She is also co-founder of the nonprofit Out of Site Center for Arts Education. Her interests include the use of contemporary art practices in the classroom and bringing student learning beyond conventional school walls.

LYNDA TREDWAY is academic coordinator of Principal Leadership Institute at the University of California, Berkeley, and founding director of the Leadership Connection for Justice in Education, and works with teacher leaders in a master's degree and administrative credential program, which incorporates the arts in its 14-month preparation program. A fabric artist herself, she implemented the BRAVO project, an arts project for aspiring leaders that focuses on the racial and equity history of California and culminates in a works-in-progress exhibition and performance each June.

ANN WETTRICH, co-director of the Center for Art and Public Life at the California College of the Arts, directs the teacher education program certifying subject matter competency in the visual arts, while providing a foundational understanding of art education. She serves on numerous community advisory boards and chairs the Teaching and Learning Oversight Committee for the Alameda County Office of Education's Alliance for Arts Learning Leadership and the Art Education Committee for the Alameda County Arts Commission.

REBECCA WHEAT, EdD, holds a doctorate in educational psychology from the University of California, Berkeley. She has been a teacher, principal, and college instructor for over 32 years. Presently she is a field supervisor at the Principal Leadership Institute, University of California, Berkeley. She is the author of articles and 3 books (*Diversity in Day Care: Options and Issues*; *The Spirited Principal*; and her recent book, *Success for Boys in School: Excellence and Exuberance*). She lives in Berkeley with her husband.

SARAH WILLNER has explored, taught, coached, and collaborated in music and music integration with students, teachers, and administrators in the Oakland public schools since 1998. She is a professional violist, as well as a performer of the music, dance, and theater of Bali, with local ensembles Gamelan Sekar Jaya and ShadowLight Productions.

PATTY YANCEY, PhD, is a professor in the school of Education, and Director of the Office of Diversity and Inclusion at Humboldt State University in Arcata, California. She teaches in the Elementary Education Credential Program and in the MA in Education Program. Her research interests include arts education, alternative public schools, and diversity in higher education.

Index